EXPRESS
SOURCEBOOK

**Practice Workshops
and Minilessons
for the Proofreader's Guide**

TE

. . . a resource of student
workshops, minilessons, and
activities to accompany

WRITERS

EXPRESS

WRITE SOURCE®

GREAT SOURCE EDUCATION GROUP
a Houghton Mifflin Company
Wilmington, Massachusetts

A Few Words About the Level 4 SourceBook

Before you begin . . .

You need to know that the SourceBook should be used with the *Writers Express* handbook, which provides information, examples, and models. The SourceBook provides your students with opportunities to practice the editing and proofreading skills presented in the handbook. SourceBook activities are organized into Practice Workshops, Minilessons, and Check-It-Out Daily Sentences.

Practice Workshops

The Practice Workshops cover what students need to know to become better writers and proofreaders. The workshop topics appear in the same order in the SourceBook as they do in the Proofreader's Guide in the *Writers Express* handbook. In each workshop, The First Step introduces the basic idea and directs students to the handbook pages they will want to use. Each workshop has clear directions and examples. Follow-up writing activities are explained in The Next Step.

Minilessons

Each Minilesson covers one idea from the handbook. Most minilessons can be done individually or with a partner.

Check-It-Out Daily Sentences

Check-It-Out Daily Sentences review basic writing skills. Focused Sentences help your students concentrate on one editing skill at a time. Proofreading Sentences offer several different sentence problems for students to correct. Sometimes they will add a word, write a different word, or simply cross out a word. Such practice helps them become more careful writers and better proofreaders.

Authors: Pat Sebranek and Dave Kemper

Printed in the United States of America

International Standard Book Number: 0-699-43695-X

6 7 8 9 10 -HLG- 02 01 00

Table of Contents

• Sentence Workshops

Understanding Sentences

Sentence Variety

Sentence Problems

Sentence Combining

• Language Workshops

Understanding Our Language

Nouns

Pronouns

Verbs

Adjectives and Adverbs

Other Parts of Speech

• Minilessons

Marking Punctuation

Editing for Mechanics

Checking Your Spelling and Usage

Understanding Sentences

Understanding Our Language

• Check-It-Out Sentences

Focused Sentences

• Check-It-Out Sentences

Proofreading Sentences

Practice Workshops Answer Key

The activities in this section of the SourceBook cover the basic language, editing, and proofreading skills students need to become better writers.

Name

End Punctuation 1

The First Step ● There are only three ways to end a sentence. You may use a period, a question mark, or an exclamation point. Your handbook explains when to use each of them. (See topic numbers 02, 54, and 56 in "Marking Punctuation," which starts on page 343.)

DIRECTIONS: Put the correct end punctuation—a period, a question mark, or an exclamation point—in the sentences below. You will also need to add a capital letter at the beginning of each sentence. The first sentence has been marked for you.

Animals can't speak our language. Did you know that many animals have their own languages? Dolphins "talk" by making clicking sounds. A dolphin can make as many as 700 clicks in one second. Bees "talk" by flapping their wings. They tell other bees where to find flowers.

Have you ever noticed that dogs have different kinds of barks? A dog barks one way when someone is at the door and another way when it hurts its paw.

Although animals can't speak English, a few can learn sign language. A gorilla named Koko knows sign language. When a kitten bit Koko, he made signs to say, "Teeth visit gorilla." He didn't say it the way you would say it, but you know what he meant. Ouch!

End Punctuation 1

The Next Step ● Write a paragraph about different ways that human beings communicate with animals. Try to use different kinds of end punctuation in your paragraph.

_____

_____

_____

_____

_____

_____

_____

_____

_____

_____

_____

_____

_____

_____

End Punctuation 2

The First Step ● This workshop activity gives you more practice using **end punctuation**. (See rules 02, 54, and 56 in "Marking Punctuation," which starts on page 343.)

DIRECTIONS: Put the correct end punctuation in the sentences below. You'll also need to add a capital letter at the beginning of each sentence. The first sentence has been marked for you.

M
many years ago, a cat named Napoleon became famous. **D** do you know why? **?I** it's because he could predict the weather.

Napoleon lived in Baltimore with his owner. **I** in the summer of 1930, it didn't rain for a long time. **O** one day, Napoleon's owner called the newspapers and said that rain was on the way. **T** they didn't believe him, but Napoleon's owner knew better. Napoleon was napping with one front paw stretched out and his head on the floor. **W** whenever Napoleon did that, it soon began to rain.

W
what do you think happened? **?Y** yes, **!I** it poured and poured. **(or) ! F** from then on, the newspapers printed Napoleon's weather forecasts. **H** he was right as often as the human weather forecaster. **D** don't you wish you had a cat like Napoleon at your house? **?**

End Punctuation 2

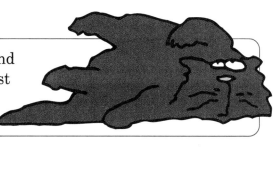

The Next Step ● People often ask questions and make comments about the weather. Write at least five sentences related to the weather. Be sure to use the correct end punctuation!

_____

_____

_____

_____

_____

_____

_____

_____

_____

_____

_____

_____

_____

_____

_____

Using Commas 1

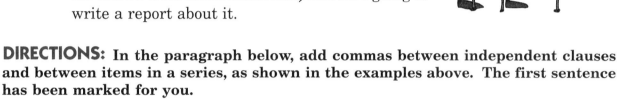

The First Step ● **Commas** are used between words or phrases in a series. Commas are also used between two independent clauses that are joined by words such as *and, but, so,* and *yet.* (See handbook page 345, topic numbers 12 and 16.)

Commas in a Series
I know someone who has pen pals in Australia, Greece, and Ireland.

Comma Between Two Independent Clauses
He knows a lot about Australia, and he's going to write a report about it.

DIRECTIONS: In the paragraph below, add commas between independent clauses and between items in a series, as shown in the examples above. The first sentence has been marked for you.

Australia is the sixth-largest country in the world, and it is the only country that takes up a whole continent. It is in the South Pacific, and it has the world's largest coral reef. The reef is called the Great Barrier Reef, and it is 1,200 miles long. Kangaroos, kookaburras, and dingoes are just a few of the unusual animals that live in Australia. Australia is only slightly smaller than the United States, but it has a lot fewer people. Australia has diamonds, gold, copper, and other gems and minerals.

Using Commas 1

The Next Step ● Write four sentences of your own about Australia or about another country. Use at least four commas.

_____

_____

_____

_____

_____

_____

_____

_____

_____

_____

_____

_____

Using Commas 2

> **The First Step** ● **Commas** are used between words or phrases in a series. Commas are also used between two independent clauses, which are joined by words such as *and, but, or, so,* and *yet.* (See handbook page 345, topic numbers 12 and 16. Also see the examples below.)

Commas in a Series
I have seen elephants at the zoo**,** at the circus**,** and at a wild animal park.

Comma Between Two Independent Clauses
My uncle's job is to take care of the elephants at the zoo**,** so he knows a lot about elephants.

DIRECTIONS: In the sentences below, add commas between independent clauses and between items in a series, as shown in the examples above. The first sentence has been marked for you.

You may think of elephants as huge, heavy, and clumsy, but did you know that they can do some pretty amazing things?

Everyone knows that elephants use their trunks to hold things, take up water, and throw dust, but some elephants use their trunks to draw things. Siri, an elephant that lived in a zoo, held a rock in her trunk, and she used it to draw designs on the floor of her cage. The zookeeper gave Siri a pencil and paper, and she kept drawing.

Everyone knows that elephants travel together in herds, and the oldest female is the leader of the herd. But few people know this story: When one baby elephant got hurt, the whole herd followed the leader for two miles to a park ranger's office. They got the ranger to follow them back, and he helped the baby elephant.

Using Commas 2

The Next Step ● Now write your own "Everyone knows . . ." story about a dog, cat, monkey, or other animal. Your story can be real or imagined. (Use two or more commas in your story.)

_____

_____

_____

_____

_____

_____

_____

_____

_____

_____

_____

_____

_____

_____

Using Commas 3

The First Step ● **Commas** *again*! Well, commas are important! You'll be using them for the rest of your life, so it's important to use them right! Remember, if you made any mistakes using commas in the last activity, try to understand why before you do this activity.

DIRECTIONS: **In the sentences below, add commas between independent clauses and between items in a series. The first sentence has been marked for you.**

Hundreds of years ago, the whole United States was covered with forests, grassy fields, and deserts. Animals lived everywhere! But there are more people today, and humans have built homes, shopping malls, and parking lots where animals used to live. Many wild birds, squirrels, and raccoons have been squeezed out of their homes.

There are some things you can do to make animals feel at home in your neighborhood. If you have a cat, put a bell on its collar, or it may sneak up on wild animals. Put water in a birdbath, pie pan, or other shallow container for birds. Plant a berry bush, and it will provide food for wild animals. Buy a bat house at the hardware store. Bats will "sleep in" during the day, but they'll be busy eating mosquitoes, flies, and other insects at night.

Using Commas 3

The Next Step ● Ask a classmate to tell you about an experience he or she had with a wild animal (not a pet). Write a paragraph about your classmate's experience. Be sure to use commas correctly!

Commas and Clauses

The First Step ● In this workshop, you'll practice another way to use **commas**: to set off long phrases and clauses. See topic number 23 on page 346 in your handbook.

DIRECTIONS: Each sentence below starts with a long phrase or clause that modifies the rest of the sentence. Add a comma after each phrase or clause. The first sentence has been done for you.

1. If you're serious about helping the environment, you can recycle many things besides paper.

2. Because glass never wears out, it can be recycled forever.

3. You may find this hard to believe, but people have been recycling glass for over 3,000 years!

4. Once worth more than gold, aluminum is a good thing to recycle.

5. At almost all recycling stations, you'll find a bin for aluminum cans.

6. It's not always easy, but plastic can be recycled, too.

7. Before you do anything else, you have to separate different kinds of plastic.

8. To avoid polluting the environment, your parents can recycle the oil and antifreeze from their cars.

9. Speaking of your parents and their cars, tires can be recycled also.

10. While you're at it, tell your parents that even their cars' old batteries can be recycled.

Commas and Clauses

_____

_____

_____

_____

_____

_____

_____

_____

_____

_____

_____

_____

_____

_____

Commas and End Punctuation Review

The First Step ● This workshop activity is a review of the two kinds of punctuation you've practiced so far: commas and end punctuation marks.

DIRECTIONS: Put commas and the correct end punctuation in the sentences below. Also capitalize the first letter of each sentence. The first sentence has been done for you.

*H*ave you ever seen turtles in pet shops, in the streets, or in parks? *T*hey were probably box turtles. *S*ome cities have street signs that warn drivers not to run over turtles—because turtles take their time. *T*here are many different kinds of turtles. *T*here are sea turtles, desert turtles, snapping turtles, and others. *S*ea turtles are huge, and they can live for 100 years. *D*esert turtles could become extinct soon because cows are eating their homes. *T*hey live under shrubs that cows like to eat. *C*an you guess how snapping turtles got their name? *T*hey will try to bite you when they're afraid, *S*o watch out!

Commas and End Punctuation Review

The Next Step ● Turtles often get turned over on their backs when they try to climb up on something. They can't get right side up again unless someone helps them. Pretend that you're a turtle, and you're stuck on your back. Write a paragraph about how you feel before and after a human comes along and helps you back onto your feet. Be sure to use each of the three types of end punctuation at least once, and add commas where they are needed.

Using Apostrophes

The First Step ● **Apostrophes** are used in many different ways. One of the most common uses is making contractions. Read about contractions in your handbook. (See page 349, topic number 43.) Then complete the following activity.

DIRECTIONS: In the following sentences, make as many contractions as you can. The first contraction has been made for you. (The number of contractions you can make is identified after each sentence.)

1. *It's*
   It is easy to get the Arctic and Antarctica mixed up. (1)

2. *They're*
   They are both frozen! (1)

3. *there's*
   But there is a way to remember which is which. (1)

4. The Arctic is an ocean *that's* that is surrounded by land, and it is *it's* at the North
   Pole. (2)

5. Antarctica is land *that's* that is surrounded by water, and it is *it's* at the South Pole. (2)

6. Polar bears and seals live on islands of ice in the Arctic, and *they're* they are at
   home there even though it is *it's* cold. (2)

7. Antarctica is even colder than the Arctic, but the penguins that live there
   don't do not seem to mind. (1)

8. Humans only visit Antarctica; they *don't* do not live there. (1)

9. The two places have one thing in common: The sun *doesn't* does not rise in either
   place for six months of the year. (1)

Using Apostrophes

The Next Step ● Pretend you are an explorer in the Antarctic. Write a message to a friend telling him or her about your trip. Use as many contractions as you can.

_____

_____

_____

_____

_____

_____

_____

_____

_____

_____

_____

_____

Making Possessives

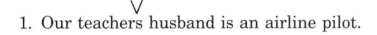

The First Step ● One important way you use **apostrophes** is to make possessives. Review page 349 in your handbook, topic numbers 45, 46, and 47.

DIRECTIONS: Each sentence below contains one or two possessive nouns that need an apostrophe (or an apostrophe *and* an "s"). Add what's needed to make the possessive form correct. The first sentence has been done for you.

1. Our teachers͈ husband is an airline pilot.

2. My sisters͈ puppy and my brothers͈ cat tease each other.

3. My fathers͈ boss is from Singapore.

4. Aunt Doris͈ hat flew out the window, and Moms͈ scarf went right after it.

5. Uncle Ross͈ʼs laughter could be heard around the block.

6. The bus͈ʼs tires ran over the hat and squashed it.

7. The boys͈ soccer team beat the girls͈ soccer team.

8. At the zoo, the elephants͈ cages are huge.

9. The snakes͈ cages are made of glass.

10. All of my classmates͈ art projects are on display.

11. I think Michelles͈ project is the best.

Making Possessives

> **The Next Step** ● Write down the names of four people you know. Imagine that each of them has caught a fish; add an apostrophe and the word "fish" to each name. Then think of four pairs of people, and write them under "Plural Possessives." Add an apostrophe and the word "fish" to each of these pairs. The first has been done for you.

Singular Possessives

1. *Joe's fish* _____

2. _____

3. _____

4. _____

5. _____

Plural Possessives

1. *Joe and Rosa's fish* _____

2. _____

3. _____

4. _____

5. _____

Using Quotation Marks 1

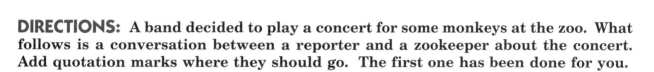

The First Step ● When you talk, it's easy to tell who is saying what. You can hear each person's voice. But when you write, you have to show when people start talking and when they stop. That's what **quotation marks** do. They come before and after the exact words someone says. Read about quotation marks in your handbook before you begin this activity. (See page 350, topic numbers 48-50.)

DIRECTIONS: A band decided to play a concert for some monkeys at the zoo. What follows is a conversation between a reporter and a zookeeper about the concert. Add quotation marks where they should go. The first one has been done for you.

"Why would a band want to play for monkeys?" the reporter asked.

"They wanted to see what the monkeys would do," answered the zookeeper.

"Well, what did the monkeys do?" asked the reporter. "Did they like the music?"

"They couldn't stand it," the zookeeper said. "One brave chimp tried to take away the bandleader's trombone to make him stop playing!"

"Did he stop?" asked the reporter.

"Yes," the zookeeper said. "The band changed to a slow, quiet song, and the monkeys sat down."

Using Quotation Marks 1

The Next Step ● Remember the last time you talked to a friend or family member about music. Write down a few sentences that each of you said. You probably won't remember the exact words, but come as close as you can! Be sure to use quotation marks correctly! Remember to start a new paragraph each time you change speakers.

_____

_____

_____

_____

_____

_____

_____

_____

_____

_____

_____

_____

_____

_____

Using Quotation Marks 2

The First Step ● Here's some practice using **quotation marks** to punctuate direct quotations. Remember, your handbook has the information you need on page 350.

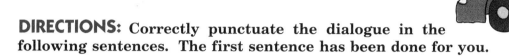

DIRECTIONS: Correctly punctuate the dialogue in the following sentences. The first sentence has been done for you.

"Margaret, did you already go to the recycling center?" Dad asked my sister.

"No," she answered. "I thought you went."

"Me? I went last time," Dad said.

"Uh-uh! I went last time!" Margaret insisted.

Mom said, "Why don't you both go? You can continue arguing on the way."

"Very funny," said Dad, as he gathered up the old newspapers.

"Okay. I'll get the bag of cans," Margaret said. "But we still have a problem."

"I don't want to hear it," Mom said.

"What's the problem?" Dad asked Margaret.

"Who's going next time?" Margaret asked.

Using Quotation Marks 2

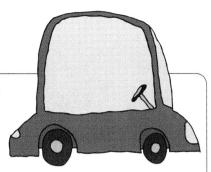

The Next Step ● Continue the story about the trip to the recycling center below. Write at least four more sentences. Be sure to use quotation marks and commas correctly. Start a new paragraph for each new speaker.

_____

_____

_____

_____

_____

_____

_____

_____

_____

_____

_____

_____

_____

Using Capital Letters 1

The First Step ● The basic rules for using **capital letters** are pretty simple: Capitalize the first letter of a sentence and all proper nouns. But it's not always so simple to figure out which nouns are proper. It depends partly on the word and partly on how the word is used in the sentence.

DIRECTIONS: Your handbook explains the rules for capitalization on pages 352-354. This activity gives you practice using the rules in topic numbers 63, 65, 67, and 74. Use those rules to find, and change the words that should be capitalized. The first sentence has been marked for you.

1. My uncle took me and my brother to see the $\overset{S}{s}$t. $\overset{L}{l}$ouis $\overset{C}{c}$ardinals play baseball.

2. The game was at $\overset{B}{b}$usch $\overset{S}{s}$tadium in $\overset{S}{s}$t. $\overset{L}{l}$ouis.

3. It was a $\overset{S}{s}$aturday game in $\overset{J}{j}$uly.

4. The $\overset{C}{c}$ardinals played the $\overset{C}{c}$incinnati $\overset{R}{r}$eds.

5. My uncle said there was another game on $\overset{S}{s}$unday.

6. My brother said he didn't think $\overset{M}{m}$other would let us go; she wanted us to go with her to $\overset{S}{s}$pringfield, $\overset{I}{i}$llinois.

7. But I said that maybe $\overset{U}{u}$ncle could get $\overset{M}{m}$om to let us go to the game instead.

8. Then our uncle said he'd invite $\overset{M}{m}$om and $\overset{D}{d}$ad to the game, too.

Using Capital Letters 1

The Next Step ● Write a paragraph about a game, concert, or other event you attended. (Or, write about one you'd like to attend!) Include as much information as you can about when and where it was, what teams or performers you saw, etc. Be sure to capitalize correctly!

_____

_____

_____

_____

_____

_____

_____

_____

_____

_____

_____

_____

_____

_____

_____

Using Capital Letters 2

The First Step ● In this activity, you'll practice using more of the rules for **capitalization**. Review your handbook's section on capitalization (pages 352-354), especially topic numbers 66, 68, 70, 75, and 76.

DIRECTIONS: In each sentence below, there are two words or phrases that should be capitalized but are not. Make the needed corrections. The first sentence has been done for you.

1. President Clinton, *S*senator Helms, *G*governor Wilson, and the governor of Oregon gave speeches.

2. Two senators, *V*vice *P*president Gore, and *M*mayor Daly held a news conference in Chicago.

3. We are studying the *D*dark *A*ages and the *M*middle *A*ages.

4. Many people confuse the *D*declaration of *I*independence and the U.S. *C*constitution.

5. The *A*american *R*red *C*cross and the *U*united *W*way helped people after the earthquake.

6. The *S*sierra *C*club and *G*greenpeace are groups that help the environment.

7. My neighbor is *S*south *A*african, and she speaks *E*english with an accent.

8. In India, most people are either *H*hindu or *M*muslim.

9. Our school got a new *X*xerox copier and some new *A*apple computers.

Using Capital Letters 2

The Next Step ● Write five sentences about a historical event you have studied in school. Be sure to include the full names of the people and places involved in the event. Trade with a partner who has done the same thing, and check each other's capitalization.

1. _____

_____

_____

2. _____

_____

_____

3. _____

_____

_____

4. _____

_____

_____

5. _____

_____

_____

Using Plurals 1

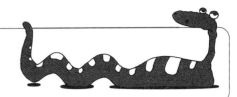

The First Step ● Page 355 of your handbook explains **plurals** and the rules for making them. Open your handbook to that page to do this activity.

DIRECTIONS: Write the plural form of each word listed below. Use the rules explained in topic numbers 77, 78, and 82.

1. fox   *foxes*

2. beach   *beaches*

3. class   *classes*

4. horse   *horses*

5. cow   *cows*

6. spider   *spiders*

7. pony   *ponies*

8. fly   *flies*

9. turkey   *turkeys*

10. bush   *bushes*

The Next Step ● Now write a short tall tale, using as many of these words in your story as you can. (Share your story with a classmate.)

Using Plurals 2

The First Step ● Making plurals isn't always as simple as adding an "s" to the end of a word. On page 355, your handbook lists eight rules for making plurals. In this activity, you'll practice almost all of them.

DIRECTIONS: Make all of the following words plural. First find the rule on page 355 you should use; then list the rule number on the first part of the line. Then, follow the rule to make the plural. The first one has been done for you.

1. lady	82	ladies
2. bush	78	bushes
3. potato	79	potatoes
4. handful	80	handfuls
5. portfolio	79	portfolios
6. monkey	82	monkeys
7. wolf	81	wolves
8. boss	78	bosses
9. baby	82	babies

10. tomato	79	tomatoes
11. lunch	78	lunches
12. mess	78	messes
13. activity	82	activities
14. leaf	81	leaves
15. child	84	children
16. chef	81	chefs
17. push	78	pushes
18. horse	77	horses

The Next Step ● Working in groups, think of nouns that are made plural under each of the rules on page 355 in your handbook. Write down at least one word for each rule. (Important: Don't use any words listed above or in your handbook!)

77	adding just s
78	ending in sh, ch, x, s, and z
79	ending in o
80	ending in ful

81	ending in f or fe
82	ending in y
83	compound nouns
84	irregular nouns

Using Numbers

The First Step ● When you use numbers in math, you always write them as numerals. But when you use numbers in your writing, sometimes they are written as words. This activity gives you practice using the rules for when to write numbers as words.

DIRECTIONS: In the sentences below, all the numbers are written as words. Some of them should be written as numerals. Open your handbook to page 356. Using the rules in topic numbers 85, 87, and 88, find the numbers that should be written as numerals, and change them. The first sentence has been marked for you.

1. There are three kids in our family, and our ages are ~~nine~~ *9*, ~~eleven~~ *11*, and ~~thirteen~~ *13*.

2. My sister's cat had six kittens; she's trying to sell them for ~~three dollars~~ *$3.00 (or) $3* each.

3. Eight people got on the bus at ~~fourteen~~ *14* Main Street.

4. The ~~twenty-one~~ *21* people in our class all go to lunch at ~~one~~ *1:00* p.m.

5. For homework, I had to do all ~~fifteen~~ *15* problems on pages ~~three through five~~ *3-5*.

6. Movie tickets cost ~~five dollars~~ *$5.00 (or) $5*, and we need tickets for six people.

7. On April ~~seven~~ *7*, 1995, I'll be ~~ten~~ *10* years old.

8. ~~16~~ *Sixteen* kids in our class got ~~one hundred~~ *100* percent on their spelling tests.

Using Numbers

The Next Step ● Write two sentences that use numbers written as numerals, and two sentences that use numbers written as words.

Numerals

1. _____

_____

_____

2. _____

_____

_____

Words

1. _____

_____

_____

2. _____

_____

_____

Using Abbreviations

The First Step ● An abbreviation is a shorter way to write a word or phrase—a shortcut! Pages 356 and 357 of your handbook explain abbreviations and give examples.

DIRECTIONS: Find all the words that can be abbreviated, and change them to their shortened form. *Hint:* You'll take 11 shortcuts! (The first one has been done for you.)

Our neighbor, ~~Mister~~ [*Mr.*] Wilson, asked me to help him move his ~~television~~ [*TV*] set tomorrow afternoon. It's lucky I know the way to his house! I won't have to use the ~~radio detecting and ranging~~ [*radar*] set I made myself. After her tomatoes got mysterious spots on them, Mrs. Wilson said never to bring "that thing" near her garden again. Oh well. I'll bring my portable ~~compact disc~~ [*CD*] player instead.

Mr. Wilson used to work for the ~~Central Intelligence~~ [*CIA*] Agency in Washington, ~~District of Columbia~~ [*D.C. (or) DC*]. He's funny! His son is a doctor, so ~~Mister~~ [*Mr.*] Wilson calls him ~~Doctor~~ [*Dr.*] Wilson. But he calls me ~~Doctor~~ [*Dr.*] Franklin, and I'm not really a doctor. ~~Mister~~ [*Mr.*] Wilson has given me a great idea, though! I think I'll open my practice today and examine ~~Doctor~~ [*Dr.*] Doolittle, the Wilson's cat. Here, kitty, kitty!

Using Abbreviations

The Next Step ● Try writing your own humorous story using as many abbreviations as you can. Exchange stories with a partner for laughs.

_____

_____

_____

_____

_____

_____

_____

_____

_____

_____

_____

_____

_____

_____

_____

Commonly Misspelled Words

The First Step ● Pandora is using the spelling rules from "Becoming a Better Speller" (page 273 in your handbook) to begin four lists of **commonly misspelled words**. (She let them out of the box a long time ago, and they have been a plague on most writers ever since.)

DIRECTIONS: Use the list beginning on page 358 in your handbook. Add at least three words to each list below.

(Answers will vary.)

Words ending in "y" have special plurals

emergency	emergencies
Monday	Mondays
anniversary	anniversaries
country	countries
Saturday	Saturdays

Words that need their final consonants doubled

getting

swimming

finally

beginning

usually

Words that have the vowels "i" and "e" together

receive

neither

friend

audience

neighborhood

Drop silent "e" before adding a suffix (ending)

judgment

writing

argument

coming

making

Commonly Misspelled Words

The Next Step ● One way to remember the spelling of a word is to use **acrostics**. You can do this by making up sentences for difficult words. Write an acrostic sentence for each of the words below. The first one is done for you.

1. geography

   Giraffes eat old, greasy rugs and paint houses yellow.
   _____

2. athletic

   _____

   _____

   _____

3. courtesy

   _____

   _____

   _____

4. humorous

   _____

   _____

   _____

Using the Right Word 1

The First Step ● Your handbook lists many of the words that are commonly misused in writing. (See pages 362-369.) Use this section to help you complete this workshop activity.

DIRECTIONS: If an underlined word is incorrect, cross it out and write the correct form above it. The first one has been done for you. (Do not change a word that is correct.)

Have you ever heard ~~you're~~ *your* parents or friends say, "It's the real McCoy"?

If you have, did you ever wonder how the saying began?

It began with a man named Elijah McCoy, ~~that~~ *who* was born in 1844. The ~~sun~~ *son* of slaves, he became ~~a~~ *an* engineer. McCoy invented ways to make machines

work better. He invented new parts for engines, ~~breaks~~ *brakes*, and other machines.

He also invented the lawn sprinkler! By the end of his life, McCoy had no

fewer than 50 patents for things he invented.

McCoy's inventions ~~maid~~ *made* machines work so much better that no ~~won~~ *one*

wanted to buy a machine without "the McCoy system." The person selling the

machine would say: "It's the real McCoy!" Today, we use the saying to mean,

"~~Its~~ *It's* the best!"

Using the Right Word 1

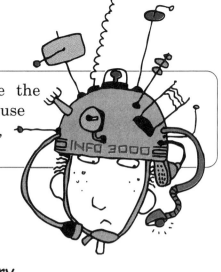

1. allowed, aloud

   We're not <u>allowed</u> to talk <u>aloud</u> in the library.
   _____

2. already, all ready
   _____

   _____

3. bring, take
   _____

   _____

4. your, you're
   _____

   _____

5. can, may
   _____

   _____

Using the Right Word 2

The First Step ● Your handbook lists many of the words that are commonly misused in writing. (See pages 362-369.) Use this section to help you complete this workshop activity.

DIRECTIONS: If the underlined word is incorrect, cross out the word and write the correct form above it. The first one has been done for you. (Do not change a word that is correct.)

        know
We don't ~~no~~ anyone who doesn't like ice cream. It can be eaten in a

     or   *There*   *a lot*
sundae ~~ore~~ in cones, sodas, and shakes. ~~Their~~ are ~~alot~~ of ice-cream flavors—

chocolate, vanilla, blueberry. Of <u>course</u>, people eat ice cream for dessert, but

some
~~sum~~ people like it for a snack.

                made   *than*
We're not sure who first ~~maid~~ ice cream. However, more ~~then~~ 700 years

                                  desserts   *By*
ago, Marco Polo brought a recipe for iced-milk ~~deserts~~ back from China. ~~Buy~~

the eighteenth century, ice cream was a very popular dessert in many <u>capital</u>

cities of the world.

Then   *an*
~~Than~~, in 1846, Nancy Johnson invented ~~a~~ ice-cream freezer. After that, ice-

             seemed   *buy*
cream factories ~~seamed~~ to open in <u>one</u> city after another. <u>So</u> we can ~~by~~ ice cream

                                     your
in stores and restaurants everywhere! What is ~~you're~~ favorite ice-cream flavor?

Using the Right Word 2

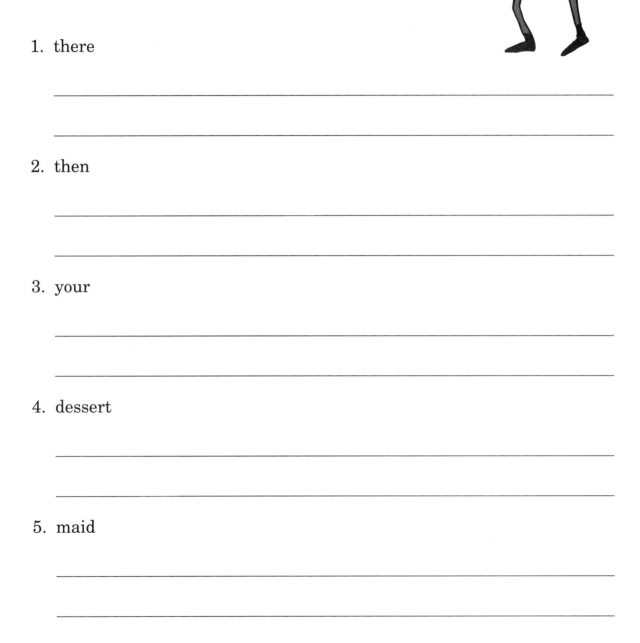

The Next Step ● Write five sentences having something to do with ice cream. Use the words listed below in the sentences.

1. there

_____

_____

2. then

_____

_____

3. your

_____

_____

4. dessert

_____

_____

5. maid

_____

_____

Using the Right Word 3

The First Step ● Your handbook lists many of the words that are commonly misused in writing. (See pages 362-369.) Use this section to help you complete this workshop activity.

DIRECTIONS: If an underlined word is incorrect, cross out the word and write the correct form above it. The first one has been done for you. (Do not change a word that is correct.)

Getting angry can cause more trouble than *it's* ~~its~~ worth! William Kennedy

learned that lesson when he *blew* ~~blue~~ his cool in a baseball game. Kennedy was

pitching for Brooklyn. He *threw* ~~through~~ a pitch that he thought was a strike. But

the umpire said it didn't *quite* ~~quiet~~ hit the strike zone. Kennedy got mad and

<u>threw</u> the ball at the umpire. It missed, but the umpire said the ball was in

play, and the base runners were *allowed* ~~aloud~~ to head for home plate! One runner

scored. That caused Brooklyn to *lose* ~~loose~~ the game. So, as you can see, *it's* ~~its~~ not *too* ~~to~~

smart to get mad. If you blow up, you could lose more than *your* ~~you're~~ cool!

Using the Right Word 3

The Next Step ● Write a short story about a time you lost your temper. Use the following five words in your story: *blew, throw, quiet, allowed, its.*

_____

_____

_____

_____

_____

_____

_____

_____

_____

_____

_____

_____

_____

_____

_____

Changing Sentence Beginnings

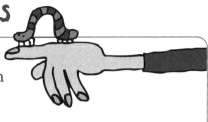

The First Step ● When you proofread your writing, you may find that too many of your sentences start with the same word. How boring! Check out "Change Your Sentence Beginnings" on page 51 in your handbook.

DIRECTIONS: Rewrite the following sentences, giving each a different beginning. The first one has been done for you.

(Answers will vary.)

1. We went to the beach on Saturday.

   On Saturday, we went to the beach.

2. We took a big umbrella to keep from getting sunburned.

   To keep from getting sunburned, we took a big umbrella.

3. We took sandwiches for lunch.

   For lunch we took sandwiches.

4. We all went into the water as soon as we got there.

   As soon as we got there, we all went into the water.

5. We played Frisbee after we ate lunch.

   After we ate lunch, we played Frisbee.

6. We had to quit when the Frisbee got lost in the ocean.

   When the Frisbee got lost in the ocean, we had to quit.

7. We left at four o'clock.

   At four o'olock we left.

8. We were all tired by the time we got home.

   By the time we got home, we were all tired.

Changing Sentence Beginnings

The Next Step ● Write a short story or personal narrative (true story) about a day at the beach, pool, or park. Then, pick two sentences from your story, and rewrite them by changing the way they begin.

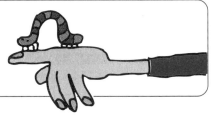

_____

_____

_____

_____

_____

_____

_____

_____

_____

_____

_____

New Sentences:

1. _____

_____

2. _____

_____

Using Powerful Words

The First Step ● When you polish your writing, make sure you've used **powerful verbs** and **specific nouns**. Page 52 of your handbook gives some examples.

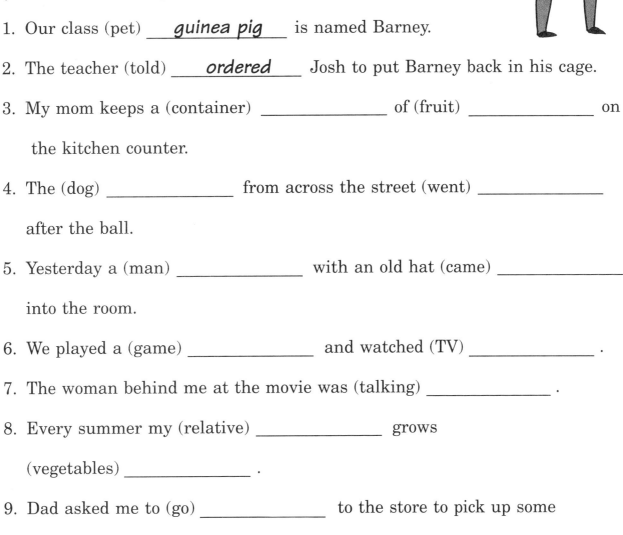

DIRECTIONS: In the sentences below, replace the nouns in parentheses with nouns that are more specific. Replace the verbs with verbs that are more powerful. The first two sentences have been done for you.

(Answers will vary.)

1. Our class (pet) ___*guinea pig*___ is named Barney.

2. The teacher (told) ___*ordered*___ Josh to put Barney back in his cage.

3. My mom keeps a (container) _____ of (fruit) _____ on

    the kitchen counter.

4. The (dog) _____ from across the street (went) _____

    after the ball.

5. Yesterday a (man) _____ with an old hat (came) _____

    into the room.

6. We played a (game) _____ and watched (TV) _____ .

7. The woman behind me at the movie was (talking) _____ .

8. Every summer my (relative) _____ grows

    (vegetables) _____ .

9. Dad asked me to (go) _____ to the store to pick up some

    (food) _____ .

Using Powerful Words

The Next Step ● Using the newspaper headline below as your starting point, write a news story. Use specific nouns and powerful verbs in your story.

Flying Saucer Lands on Playground

_____

_____

_____

_____

_____

_____

_____

_____

_____

_____

_____

_____

_____

_____

_____

_____

_____

Using Colorful Modifiers

The First Step ● **Colorful adjectives** and **adverbs** add life to your writing, and they make it real to the reader. Check out "Choose Colorful Modifiers" on page 52 in your handbook.

DIRECTIONS: In the sentences below, fill in each blank with an adjective or adverb. (Remember: Adjectives modify nouns, adverbs modify verbs.) Use colorful adjectives that tell the reader how things looked, sounded, smelled, tasted, and so on. Use adverbs that tell how the action happened.

(Answers will vary.)

My cousin took me to a carnival. It was nighttime, and the moon was

_____*bright*_____ . The _____ carnival lights

glowed. _____ music was playing _____ .

The _____ smell of popcorn was in the air. I could hear the

_____ screams of people on the _____ roller

coaster. I wanted to ride it, but I felt _____ . My heart

pounded _____ as I watched the _____ roller

coaster cars plunge down the track. My _____ cousin said,

"Let's go, kid." We got on. Our _____ car lurched forward

_____ . There was no going back. I gripped the bar

_____ with _____ hands. We chugged up a

steep section of track. From the top, the whole carnival looked

_____ and _____ . Suddenly, we were falling.

I screamed _____ and closed my eyes.

Using Colorful Modifiers

The Next Step ● Write a "sensory poem" about a time you went on a roller coaster or some other ride. In a sensory poem, you have to use sensory details that describe sights, sounds, feelings, smells, and tastes. (See handbook page 187 for more details.)

_____

_____

_____

_____

_____

_____

_____

_____

_____

_____

_____

_____

_____

_____

_____

_____

Name

Fixing Fragments 1

The First Step ● Your handbook explains different kinds of sentence errors and how to correct them. (See page 87.) This activity gives you practice correcting one kind of sentence error, **sentence fragments**.

DIRECTIONS: On each line below, put an **S** if the words that follow make a sentence. Put an **F** if they make a sentence fragment. The first one has been marked for you. (There is a total of seven fragments.)

_____ F _____ 1. the Aztecs in what is now Mexico

_____ F _____ 2. built cities during the 1200s

_____ F _____ 3. their main city parks and a zoo

_____ S _____ 4. the Aztecs used chocolate as money

_____ F _____ 5. the Maya in Central America

_____ F _____ 6. built the tallest pyramid in the New World

_____ F _____ 7. a kind of picture writing called hieroglyphs

_____ S _____ 8. the Incas lived in South America

_____ F _____ 9. built 12,000 miles of roads

_____ S _____ 10. they also built huge buildings and made pottery

Fixing Fragments 1

The Next Step ● Go back to the fragments and add words to make them complete sentences. Here's the first sentence to get you started. (Use capital letters and end punctuation.)

(Answers may vary.)

1. The Aztecs <u>lived</u> in what is now Mexico.

2. <u>They</u> built cities during the 1200s.

3. Their main city <u>had</u> parks and a zoo.

4. The Maya <u>lived</u> in Central America.

5. <u>They</u> built the tallest pyramid in the New World.

6. <u>They used</u> a kind of picture writing called hieroglyphs.

7. <u>The Incas</u> built 12,000 miles of road.

Fixing Fragments 2

The First Step ● In this activity, you'll practice correcting **sentence fragments**. See page 87 in your handbook for information about correcting sentence fragments.

DIRECTIONS: On each line below, put an **S** if the words that follow make a sentence. Put an **F** if they make a sentence fragment. The first one has been marked for you. (There is a total of six fragments.)

_____F_____   1. the Inuit people in the Arctic

_____S_____   2. the word "Inuit" means "the people"

_____F_____   3. called the Inuit "Eskimos"

_____S_____   4. some Inuit used to live in igloos in the winter

_____S_____   5. igloos were made out of blocks of ice

_____F_____   6. others huts out of whale bones

_____F_____   7. also made one-person boats called "kayaks"

_____F_____   8. larger boats called "umiaks"

_____F_____   9. made sleds that were pulled by dogs

_____S_____   10. the Inuit people have a proud tradition

Fixing Fragments 2

> **The Next Step** ● Go back to the fragments and add words to make them complete sentences. (Use correct capitalization and punctuation.) The first one has been done for you.

(Answers may vary.)

1. The Inuit people <u>live</u> in the Arctic.

   _____

2. <u>Explorers</u> called the Inuit "Eskimos."

   _____

3. Others <u>built</u> huts out of whale bones.

   _____

4. The <u>Inuit</u> also made one-person boats called "kayaks."

   _____

5. Larger boats <u>were</u> called "umiaks."

   _____

6. <u>They</u> made sleds that were pulled by dogs.

   _____

Name

Compound Subjects and Compound Verbs

The First Step ● You already know that every sentence needs a subject and a verb. But a sentence *may* have more than one subject or more than one verb. That's called a **compound subject** or **compound verb (predicate)**. Your handbook explains them on pages 86 and 371.

DIRECTIONS: Rewrite each of the following sentences two times. First, change the sentence so that it has a compound subject. Then, change the sentence so that it has a compound verb. An example has been done for you.

(Answers will vary.)

1. Our class had a pet party.

   compound subject: Our class and Mrs. Nathan's class had a pet party.

   compound verb: Our class had a pet party and learned about animals.

2. Stacy brought her iguana.

   compound subject: Stacy and Lucy brought their iguana.

   compound verb: Stacy brought her iguana and fed it.

3. Leslie baked cupcakes.

   compound subject: Leslie and her sister baked cupcakes.

   compound verb: Leslie baked cupcakes and frosted them.

4. Juan brought dog biscuits and carrots.

   compound subject: Juan and his best friend brought dog biscuits and carrots.

   compound verb: Juan brought dog biscuits and carrots and fed them to his friends' pets.

Understanding Sentences **53**

Compound Subjects and Compound Verbs

Compound subjects:

1. _____

_____

_____

2. _____

_____

_____

Compound verbs:

1. _____

_____

_____

2. _____

_____

_____

Correcting Run-On Sentences 1

The First Step ● Your handbook explains a kind of
sentence error called **run-on sentences**. (See page
87.) There are two ways to correct run-on sentences:
(1) You can add end punctuation to split the run-on
sentence into two sentences, or (2) you can add
punctuation and a connecting word to make
one correct sentence.

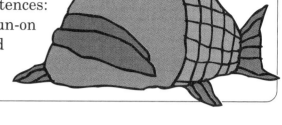

DIRECTIONS: All the sentences below are run-on sentences. Correct them by
dividing them into two sentences. Use correct capitalization and end punctuation
in your new sentences. The first one has been done for you.

1. Fish never close their eyes. They don't even blink.

2. Earthworms have 10 hearts. Snails have eyes on their feelers.

3. Grasshoppers can jump 30 inches. That's like you jumping a football
   field.

4. Ants can lift 50 times their weight. How much can you lift?

5. Squirrels bury more nuts than they dig up. The nuts left in the
   ground sometimes grow into trees.

6. Birds' wings are made of feathers. Bats' wings are made of skin.

7. Camels drink as much as 30 gallons of water at one time. No
   wonder they can cross deserts.

8. Kangaroo rats never drink water. They get the water they need from
   the plants they eat.

© Great Source. All rights reserved.

Correcting Run-On Sentences 2

The First Step ● In this activity, you'll practice correcting **run-on sentences** by adding a comma and a connecting word to make one correct sentence. Here are some connecting words you might choose from: *and, but, so,* and *yet.*

DIRECTIONS: All the sentences below are run-on sentences. Correct them by adding a comma and a connecting word. The first one has been done for you.

(Answers will vary.)

1. Black bears are the most common kind ‚ *and* they are the smallest bears, too.

2. Brown bears are the biggest bears ‚ *and* they can weigh 1,600 pounds!

3. Polar bears live in the Arctic ‚ *so* they swim in the cold ocean.

4. Their thick fur keeps them warm ‚ *and* they use their front paws as paddles.

5. There are only a few grizzly bears left ‚ *so* most live in national parks.

6. Baby bears are small enough to hold in one hand ‚ *yet* grown-up bears can be eight feet long.

7. Bears travel over a large area during summer ‚ *but* in the winter they stay in a warm den.

8. Bears can run faster than people ‚ *yet* only black bears can climb trees.

Correcting Rambling Sentences

The First Step ● Your handbook explains different kinds of sentence errors and how to correct them. (See handbook page 87.) In this activity, you'll practice correcting one kind of sentence error, **rambling sentences**.

DIRECTIONS: Below are two rambling sentences. Correct them by dividing them into as many sentences as you think are needed. Cross out the extra *and*'s, capitalize the first letter of each sentence, and use the correct end punctuation. We've shown you where we'd end the first sentence.

1. Misha and I went to the zoo yesterday. and we *We* saw polar bears, zebras, and elephants. and we *We* also saw seals and otters. and then *Then* we got some ice cream and rested for a few minutes. and finally, *Finally* we saw the baby animals in the children's zoo.

2. My mom went to Japan on a business trip. and she *She* called me as soon as she got there. and she *She* said it was already Wednesday there even though it was only Tuesday here. and I asked her how she could be in a different day and still be talking to me. and she *She* said I should ask my science teacher.

Correcting Rambling Sentences

The Next Step ● Write a short story about an unusual lunch hour. Use *and*'s instead of end punctuation so that you have one long rambling sentence. Exchange your story with a classmate, and turn this rambling sentence into several shorter sentences.

Name

Subject-Verb Agreement 1

The First Step ● Page 88 of your handbook explains **subject-verb agreement**. Basically, it means that if the subject of a sentence is singular, the verb must be singular, too; if the subject is plural, the verb must be plural, too.

DIRECTIONS: In the following sentences, the subject and verb do not agree. First figure out whether the subject is singular or plural. Then write the correct verb on the line provided so that it agrees with the subject. The first two sentences have been done for you.

1. The kids in our class has some strange pets. _____*have*_____

2. Jamila have a ferret. _____*has*_____

3. Ferrets is a lot like weasels. _____*are*_____

4. Jamila's ferret are named Gizmo. _____*is*_____

5. He run really fast. _____*runs*_____

6. Jamila's golden retriever Sam love Gizmo. _____*loves*_____

7. They takes naps together. _____*take*_____

8. Gizmo sneak up on Sam sometimes. _____*sneaks*_____

9. Then he bite Sam's ears. _____*bites*_____

10. He are just playing, though. _____*is*_____

Subject-Verb Agreement 1

The Next Step ● Write five or six sentences about an unusual pet you've known. Make sure the subjects and verbs of your sentences "agree." Then, trade papers with a classmate who's done the same thing, and check each other's sentences.

1. _____

_____

2. _____

_____

3. _____

_____

4. _____

_____

5. _____

_____

6. _____

_____

Subject-Verb Agreement 2

The First Step ● This activity gives you practice making subjects and verbs "agree." You'll practice with sentences that have compound subjects. There are two basic rules you need to know:

1. A compound subject connected by **and** needs a plural verb.
2. A compound subject connected by **or** may need a plural or singular verb. The verb agrees with the subject that's closer to it.

Note: See page 88 of your handbook for examples.

DIRECTIONS: Using the rules above, correct the following sentences by making the subject and verb agree. The first two have been done for you.

1. Michelle and Cindy ~~is~~ *are* going to start a band. *(Use rule no. 1)*

2. Either the cats or the dog ~~have~~ *has* to go out. *(Use rule no. 2)*
   The verb agrees with dog, because it's closer to the verb than cats.

3. Either Tom or Marsha ~~play~~ *plays* shortstop.

4. Dan and Amy ~~takes~~ *take* guitar lessons.

5. Chachi and Cindy ~~is~~ *are* the best singers in our school.

6. Cindy's brothers or sister usually ~~sing~~ *sings* with her.

7. Charlie's brother or sisters ~~is~~ *are* always yelling at him.

8. Jeff and Darla ~~goes~~ *go* to California every summer.

9. Sue's brothers and cousin ~~plays~~ *play* tennis.

10. Sue's brothers or cousin ~~are~~ *is* coming to pick her up.

Subject-Verb Agreement 2

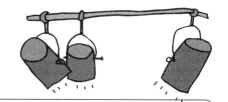

The Next Step ● Write two sentences using rule number 1 and two using rule number 2. Have a classmate check your answers.

Rule 1:

1. _____

_____

_____

_____

2. _____

_____

_____

Rule 2:

1. _____

_____

_____

2. _____

_____

_____

Name _____

Sentence Problems

The First Step ● Certain problems can sneak into your sentences right under your nose! Some of these sneaky **sentence problems** are explained on page 89 of your handbook.

DIRECTIONS: Each of the following sentences contains one of the problems discussed on page 89. Correct each sentence by crossing out or changing the problem word (write the new word on the blank provided). The first one has been done for you.

1. My brother Mark ~~he~~ loves ice cream. _____

2. My mom ~~she~~ only lets him have it after dinner. _____

3. He doesn't get ~~no~~ ice cream unless he eats all his dinner. _____*any*_____

4. He begs, but Mom says he should ~~of~~ eaten his vegetables. _____*have*_____

5. He'll say, "Harley doesn't have to eat ~~no~~ vegetables!" _____*any*_____

6. Harley ~~he's~~ our dog. _____*is*_____

7. "Harley doesn't get ~~no~~ ice cream, either!" Mom says. _____*any*_____

8. I could ~~of~~ told her that Harley *did* get ice cream once. _____*have*_____

9. Mark ~~he~~ gave it to Harley when no one was watching. _____

10. If Mark and Harley could get away with it, ~~he~~ would eat gallons of ice cream. _____*they*_____

11. If Dad and Mom catch Mark sneaking ice cream, ~~she~~ won't let him have any for a week! _____*they*_____

The Next Step ● Write three more sentences about Mark and Harley. Be careful to avoid the sentence problems you worked with above.

Making Compound Sentences

The First Step ● This workshop activity gives you practice combining sentences. You'll make **compound sentences**. Your handbook explains using compound sentences on page 93.

DIRECTIONS: Combine the following pairs of sentences into one compound sentence. Remember, use words such as *and*, *but*, and *so*— plus a comma—to make compound sentences. The first sentence has been done for you.

1. John's story was about his vacation. It was scary.

   John's story was about his vacation, and it was scary.

2. John went hiking with his uncle. John nearly stepped on a rattlesnake!

   John went hiking with his uncle, and John nearly stepped on a rattlesnake!

3. John knew he should back up slowly. He wanted to run.

   John knew he should back up slowly, but he wanted to run.

4. John kept his cool. He slowly stepped away from the snake.

   John kept his cool, and he slowly stepped away from the snake.

5. John says he's never going hiking again. His uncle says he'll change his mind.

   John says he's never going hiking again, but his uncle says he'll change his mind.

The Next Step ● On your own paper, jot down four simple sentences about your last gym class. Then exhange your work with a classmate, and see if you can combine any of your partner's ideas into compound sentences.

Combining Sentences 1

The First Step ● Too many short, choppy sentences make your writing . . . *choppy*! To smooth it out and make it more fun to read, **combine short sentences**. Pages 90-93 in your handbook tell you how.

DIRECTIONS: Combine each of these groups of sentences to make one sentence. Use a key word or series of words. See handbook page 91. The first one has been done for you.

1. Our school cafeteria is huge. Our school cafeteria is crowded. Our school cafeteria is noisy.

   Our school cafeteria is huge, crowded, and noisy.

2. You always have to wait in a line. The line is long.

   You always have to wait in a long line.

   _____

3. You're supposed to wait your turn. You're supposed to wait quietly.

   You're supposed to quietly wait your turn.

   _____

4. They always have hamburgers. They always have French fries. They always have brownies.

   They always have hamburgers, French fries, and brownies.

   _____

5. There was a food fight in the cafeteria. It was yesterday. The food fight was messy.

   There was a messy food fight in the cafeteria yesterday.

   _____

Combining Sentences 2

The First Step ● There are many ways to **combine sentences**. Page 92 of your handbook explains how to combine sentences with phrases.

DIRECTIONS: In this activity, you'll practice combining sentences with prepositional phrases and appositive phrases. One example of each has been done for you. Notice how commas are used to set off appositive phrases. (See topic number 22 on page 346 in your handbook.)

1. Mr. Gonzalez is a baseball player. He is our next-door neighbor.

   Mr. Gonzalez, our next-door neighbor, is a baseball player.

2. He plays the outfield. He plays for the Texas Rangers.

   He plays the outfield for the Texas Rangers.

3. Mrs. Fowler asked him for his autograph. She lives across the street.

   Mrs. Fowler, who lives across the street, asked him for his

   autograph.

4. He signed his name. He signed it on a baseball.

   He signed his name on a baseball.

5. He gave me two free tickets to a home game. That was right after he moved in.

   He gave me two free tickets to a home game right after he moved

   in.

6. He told me to come to the dugout. He told me to come before the game.

   He told me to come to the dugout before the game.

Combining Sentences 3

> **The First Step** ● Another way to **combine sentences** is to make complex sentences. A complex sentence is two ideas connected with a *subordinate conjunction* or a *relative pronoun.* (Check page 93 in your handbook, the section labeled "Use Complex Sentences.")

DIRECTIONS: Combine each pair of sentences below to make one complex sentence. Use the connecting word in parentheses. The first sentence has been done for you.

1. The Cherokee lived near the Great Lakes. Other tribes pushed them off their land. (until)

   The Cherokee lived near the Great Lakes until other tribes pushed them off their land.

2. They moved to the Appalachian Mountains. They became the most powerful tribe in the area. (where)

   They moved to the Appalachian Mountains where they became the most powerful tribe in the area.

3. They built more than 200 villages. Villages had 30 to 60 log houses each. (which)

   They built more than 200 villages, which had 30 to 60 log houses each.

4. The Creek lived in what is now Georgia and Alabama. They were farmers. (who)

   The Creek, who were farmers, lived in what is now Georgia and Alabama.

5. The Creek lived in villages. All of the villages had central plazas. (that)

   The Creek lived in villages that all had central plazas.

Combining Sentences 3

The Next Step ● Write five sentences about a time you traveled some place near or far. Use one of the following subordinate conjunctions in each of your sentences: *after, although, because, before, if, since, though, unless, until, when, where,* or *while.*

1. _____

_____

_____

2. _____

_____

_____

3. _____

_____

_____

4. _____

_____

_____

5. _____

_____

_____

Simple and Complete Subjects

The First Step ● The **simple subject** is the part of a sentence that is doing something. The **complete subject** is the simple subject and all the words that describe it. (See handbook page 371.) *Hint:* Sometimes the simple subject stands alone.

DIRECTIONS: In each sentence below, circle the simple subject. Then underline the complete subject. The first two sentences have been done for you.

1. (Catherine) lives in a castle not far from Paris.

2. (Roy,) Catherine's friend, built a rocket out of cat-food cans.

3. (Rocky,) a raccoon, rode Roy's rocket to the moon.

4. A moon (monster) wearing a cowboy hat roared at Rocky.

5. The hungry (monster) ate Rocky's rocket.

6. (Randy,) the flying squirrel, flew Rocky back home.

7. (Catherine) invited Randy and Rocky over to the castle for crêpes.

The Next Step ● Now write three funny sentences of your own. They don't have to be true . . . just funny! In each sentence, circle the simple subject and underline the complete subject.

1. _____ *(Answers will vary.)* _____

_____

2. _____

_____

3. _____

_____

Understanding Sentences **69**

Simple and Complete Predicates

The First Step ● The **simple predicate** (verb) is the part of a sentence that says something about the subject. The **complete predicate** is the simple predicate with all the words that describe it. (See handbook page 371.)

DIRECTIONS: In each sentence below, circle the simple predicate. Then underline the complete predicate. The first two sentences have been done for you.

1. Doug (is) my little brother.

2. He (is digging) a hole in the backyard.

3. He (plans) to dig all the way to China.

4. He (works) on the hole every day.

5. Mom (saw) the hole last Friday.

6. She (asked) Doug a lot of questions.

7. Mom (laughed) for a long time after that!

The Next Step ● Now write three sentences about your own little brother or sister, or about a friend. Circle the simple predicate, and underline the complete predicate in each sentence.

1. _____ *(Answers will vary.)* _____

_____

2. _____

_____

3. _____

_____

Types of Sentences 1

The First Step ● Page 373 of your handbook explains the three types of sentences: **simple sentences, compound sentences,** and **complex sentences**. You've already had a lot of practice with all three types. For example, when you practiced combining sentences, you created some simple sentences, some compound sentences, and some complex sentences.

DIRECTIONS: Next to each sentence below, write *simple,* *compound,* or *complex.* Two sentences have been done for you.

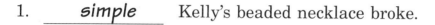

1. _____simple_____ Kelly's beaded necklace broke.

2. _____simple_____ Tomorrow I am going to start my book report.

3. _____complex_____ My best friend shares his lunch with me because he doesn't like what his dad packs.

4. _____simple_____ The gym teacher is strict, organized, and fair.

5. _____compound_____ My puppy has hair hanging down over her eyes, and she looks just like a dust mop.

6. _____compound_____ Our dog likes to eat shoes, but he won't touch my brother's smelly slippers.

7. _____simple_____ Tom and Mary danced around the room.

8. _____simple_____ John slipped on the ice and fell on his rear end.

9. _____simple_____ The dog was friendly, playful, and smart.

10. _____simple_____ Our cat curls up on top of my homework.

11. _____complex_____ Very cold weather, which came down from northern Canada, closed school for a day.

The Next Step ● Write five sentences about one or more of the favorite things you have displayed on the wall in your bedroom. Next to each sentence, identify the type of sentences you used.

Types of Sentences 2

The First Step ● Learning the three types of sentences takes practice. Review page 373 of your handbook, which explains **simple, compound,** and **complex** sentences.

DIRECTIONS: Look at the student speech "Lansing, My Hometown" on page 281 in your handbook. On the lines below, write *simple, compound,* or *complex* to identify each sentence. A few have been done for you.

1. Hello.   *simple*

2. My name is Angela Zischke.   *simple*

3. I have lived in Lansing, Michigan, my whole life
   (10 years), and all of it has been great.   *compound*

4. There are a lot of places to visit that are fun, but
   my personal favorite is the capitol.   *compound*

5. The capitol is educational and fun at the same time.   *simple*

6. It has just been restored and was rededicated on
   November 19, 1992.   *simple*

7. There now is a lot of history in the building, which
   makes it a lot more interesting.   *complex*

8. For instance, they have Civil War flags on the bottom
   floor where you look up at the dome.   *complex*

9. In the dome there are beautiful paintings of goddesses
   and the past governors of our state.   *simple*

10. There are also beautiful chandeliers.   *simple*

11. The stairs are lined with many wonderful wood carvings.   *simple*

72 *Understanding Sentences*

Kinds of Sentences

The First Step ● **Declarative sentences** make statements. **Interrogative sentences** ask questions. **Imperative sentences** give commands. **Exclamatory sentences** show emotion. (See handbook page 373.)

Examples:

Declarative	The velveteen rabbit is soft and cuddly.
Interrogative	Does the boy really think his rabbit is alive?
Imperative	Get rid of the sick boy's toys.
Exclamatory	Look at those rabbits dancing!

DIRECTIONS: Write four sentences (one of each kind) about a favorite stuffed animal or toy you remember especially well. Use the examples above as models.

Declarative

(Answers will vary.)

_____

_____

Interrogative

_____

_____

Imperative

_____

_____

Exclamatory

_____

_____

Kinds of Sentences

The Next Step ● Exchange sentences with a partner. Check to see that your classmate has written an example of each of the four kinds of sentences. Then, if you enjoyed thinking about your stuffed animal, write a story about it.

_____

_____

_____

_____

_____

_____

_____

_____

_____

_____

_____

_____

_____

Kinds of Nouns

> **The First Step** ● A **common noun** is the general name of a person, a place, a thing, or an idea. A **proper noun** is a particular name of a person, a place, a thing, or an idea. Use capital letters for proper nouns. (See handbook page 375.)

DIRECTIONS: Write a common noun to go with each proper noun. Then write a proper noun to go with each common noun.

Proper Nouns	Common Nouns
1. Milwaukee	*city*
2. Florida	*state*
3. Pacific	*ocean*
4. Sunday	*day*
5. October	*month*
6. Bozo	*clown*
7. *Jim* *(Answers will vary.)*	boy
8. _____	river
9. _____	team
10. _____	athlete
11. _____	school
12. _____	lake

Kinds of Nouns

The Next Step ● Now write five sentences. Use a common and a proper noun in each one. Mark each common noun with a **C** and each proper noun with a **P.**

Example: $\overset{P}{\text{Washington}}$ was our first $\overset{C}{\text{president.}}$

1. _____

_____

_____

2. _____

_____

_____

3. _____

_____

_____

4. _____

_____

_____

5. _____

_____

_____

Singular and Plural Nouns

The First Step ● A **singular noun** names one person, place, thing, or idea. A **plural noun** names more than one person, place, thing, or idea. (See handbook page 375.)

Singular	marker	shoe	student	recess	game
Plural	markers	shoes	students	recesses	games

DIRECTIONS: Write a humorous paragraph about a recent school activity. To get started, you might want to use some of the words above. When you are finished, mark each plural noun with a **P** and each singular noun with an **S**.

Your Paragraph

(Answers will vary.)

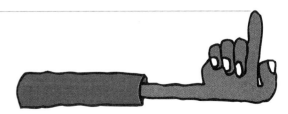

Uses of Nouns

The First Step ● A **subject noun** is a noun that does something or is being talked about. A **predicate noun** is a noun that renames the subject. It is linked to the subject by a linking verb. A **possessive noun** is a noun used to show possession or ownership. (See handbook page 376 for samples.)

DIRECTIONS: Use the sentences in your handbook as models, and write your own sentences below.

Write two sentences using *subject nouns*. Underline and label them.

1. _____ (Answers will vary.) _____

2. _____

Write two sentences using *predicate nouns*. Underline and label them.

1. _____ (Answers will vary.) _____

2. _____

Write two sentences using *possessive nouns*. Underline and label them.

1. _____ (Answers will vary.) _____

2. _____

Nouns As Objects

> **The First Step** ● When you think of nouns, you probably think of them as the subjects of sentences.
>
>   **Examples:** The **cat** chased the dog.
>   The **ball** rolled into the street.
>
> But nouns may also be used as **objects**. In the examples above, "dog" and "street" are objects. Page 376 in your handbook explains nouns used as objects.

DIRECTIONS: Each sentence below has at least one noun used as an object. Underline each object. Above the object, write what *kind* of object it is: direct object, indirect object, or object of a preposition. One example of each kind of object has been done for you.
Hint: Four sentences have both a direct object and an indirect object, and one sentence has both a direct object and an object of a preposition.

               direct object
1. Joey called the <u>police</u>.

         indirect object   *direct object*
2. The teacher gave <u>Julie</u> a <u>pencil</u>.

              object of preposition
3. Mom parked behind the <u>school</u>.

            direct object
4. We built a <u>playhouse</u>.

              direct object
5. Mom painted our <u>house</u>.

        indirect object   *direct object*
6. Last night I read <u>Brad</u> a <u>story</u>.

       indirect object   *direct object*
7. Rene gave <u>Michael</u> a <u>cookie</u>.

  indirect object   *direct object*
8. Darla sent <u>me</u> a <u>valentine</u>.

         direct object   *object of preposition*
9. Gerardo made a <u>speech</u> in our <u>class</u>.

        indirect object   *direct object*
10. Angel brought <u>everyone</u> an <u>eraser</u>.

Nouns As Objects

The Next Step ● Choose any three of the sentences. Rewrite them so that the noun that is now the subject of the sentence is used as an object in the new sentence. The first one has been done for you.

                                  subject
Original sentence: Joey called the police.
                                              object
1. **New sentence:** *The police called Joey.*

2. **New sentence:** _____

   _____

   _____

3. **New sentence:** _____

   _____

   _____

4. **New sentence:** _____

   _____

   _____

Uses of Personal Pronouns

> **The First Step** ● A **subject pronoun** is used as the subject of a sentence. An **object pronoun** is used after an action verb or in a prepositional phrase. A **possessive pronoun** shows ownership. To learn more about this, carefully read through the sample sentences and the information about personal pronouns listed on page 377 of your handbook.

DIRECTIONS: Turn to page 76 in your handbook and read the model essay. With a partner, search for personal pronouns in the essay. *In the order in which you find them,* write the pronouns in the correct box below. *Hint*: There are 21 personal pronouns in the model, including the one in the title.

Subject Pronouns

Singular	she, I, I, It, It, It, it, you
Plural	we, We, we

Object Pronouns

Singular	it, her
Plural	them, them

Possessive Pronouns

Singular	My, my, My, my
Plural	our, our

Name

Uses of Personal Pronouns

The Next Step ● Write a paragraph about something your community is doing to help the environment. Exchange your paragraph with a classmate, and circle all the pronouns. Then put each pronoun into the correct box below.

Subject Pronouns

Singular		Plural	

Object Pronouns

Singular		Plural	

Possessive Pronouns

Singular		Plural	

The Person of a Pronoun 1

The First Step ● The **person of a pronoun** tells you whether the pronoun represents a person who is speaking, a person being spoken to, or a person or thing that is being spoken about. (See page 378 in your handbook.)

	First-Person Pronoun Represents Person Speaking	**Second-Person Pronoun** Represents Person Being Spoken To	**Third-Person Pronoun** Represents Person or Thing Being Spoken About
Singular	I	you	he, she, it
Plural	we	you	they

DIRECTIONS: In the sentences below, fill in each blank with the correct pronoun from the table above. The first two have been done for you.

Blue whales are the biggest animals that ever lived. _____*They*_____ are even bigger than dinosaurs! _____*They*_____ weigh as much as 10 school buses, and _____*they*_____ have hearts as big as cars.

_____*I*_____ have a friend named Jerry, who went out on a boat to see whales in the ocean. _____*They*_____ have to come to the surface to breathe. Jerry said _____*he*_____ saw four whales. _____*He*_____ said _____*they*_____ slap their tails on the water, just for fun. _____*He*_____ said that one whale was so close to the boat that when _____*it*_____ slapped its tail, water splashed on him.

A whale expert named Tasha was on the boat. _____*She*_____ told Jerry that whales eat one ton of food every day. _____*I*_____ told Jerry I didn't believe it. _____*He*_____ answered, "If _____*you*_____ saw how big _____*they*_____ are, you'd believe it!"

The Person of a Pronoun 2

The First Step ● Your handbook explains **person of a pronoun** on page 378. Review it before doing this practice activity.

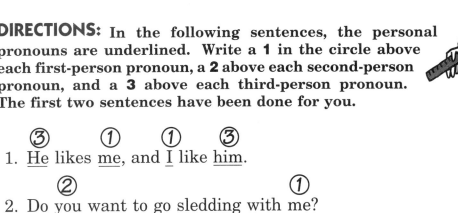

DIRECTIONS: In the following sentences, the personal pronouns are underlined. Write a **1** in the circle above each first-person pronoun, a **2** above each second-person pronoun, and a **3** above each third-person pronoun. The first two sentences have been done for you.

1. ③He likes ①me, and ①I like ③him.

2. Do ②you want to go sledding with ①me?

3. ①We had hot cocoa, and ③they built a snowman.

4. ③They put a hat on ③its head.

5. Where did ②you and ③he go?

6. Is ③she going with ②you or with ①me?

7. ②You and ①I should go in ③their car.

8. ③They don't know where ③his house is.

9. ③She borrowed the sled from ③him because ③he wasn't using ③it.

10. ②You can return ③it to ①us or to ③them.

11. Is ①our sled in ②your car or in ③their car?

Types of Verbs 1

The First Step ● There are three types of **verbs,** right? ("Check It Out" in your handbook on page 380.) Action verbs tell what the subject is doing. Linking verbs link a subject to a noun or an adjective. Helping verbs help state an action or show time.

DIRECTIONS: Without looking in your handbook, jot down as many verbs for each type as you can in 5 minutes! When your time is up, use the explanations in your handbook to check your verbs.

Action Verbs	Linking Verbs	Helping Verbs
	(Answers will vary.)	

Types of Verbs 1

The Next Step ● Write a story about preparing and eating your favorite food. Underline and label the verbs in your story: A (action), L (linking), or H (helping). Share your work with a classmate.

Types of Verbs 2

The First Step ● There are three types of verbs: **action verbs**, **linking verbs**, and **helping verbs**. They're explained on page 380 of your handbook.

DIRECTIONS: The paragraphs below were copied from a model story that appears on page 174 of your handbook. All the verbs are underlined. Above each verb, label it *action*, *linking*, or *helping*. Two verbs have been labeled for you.

      action   *helping* *action* **action**
"Get down, Antonio. They will see you. Get down."

       helping *action*   *linking*
Everything was happening so fast. Captain Magellan was dead, the crew

helping *action*   *linking*
had scattered into the woods, and now we were under attack.

        action   *linking*   *linking*
"Juan," whispered Antonio. "Since the captain is dead, you are now in

       helping *action*
charge. You must get us out of here."

       linking   *linking*
Yes, Antonio was right. I, Juan Sebastian del Cano, was in charge. But

action
get us out of here? How?

Types of Verbs 2

The Next Step ● Continue the story about Antonio and Juan Sebastian del Cano. What will happen to them? Where will they go? Afterward, underline and label the verbs: A (action), L (linking), or H (helping). Share your work with a classmate.

_____

_____

_____

_____

_____

_____

_____

_____

_____

_____

_____

_____

_____

_____

_____

_____

_____

_____

Singular and Plural Verbs

The First Step ● A **singular verb** must be used when the subject in a sentence is singular. A **plural verb** must be used when the subject is plural. (See handbook page 381.)

DIRECTIONS: Give a name to each of the kids below. Then write a sentence about each of them, using one of these singular verbs: **looks, wishes, waits, hopes, stares, listens, wonders, tries, keeps, sees,** and **smiles.** We've done the first one for you.

1. *Marty stares at the hamster in the cage.*

   (Answers will vary.)

2. _____

   _____

   _____

3. _____

   _____

4. _____

   _____

5. _____

   _____

Marty

Singular and Plural Verbs

The Next Step ● Write three sentences with the word *kids* as the subject. Use one of these plural verbs in each of your sentences: *wonder, hope,* and *see.*

1. _____

   _____

   _____

   _____

   _____

2. _____

   _____

   _____

   _____

   _____

3. _____

   _____

   _____

   _____

   _____

Irregular Verbs 1

The First Step ● To make most verbs past tense, all you do is add "ed" to the end. Easy. But then there are **irregular verbs**. They're called *irregular* because you don't make them past tense in the *regular* way. Your handbook explains irregular verbs on pages 381 and 382.

DIRECTIONS: Study the chart of irregular verbs on page 382. Then close your handbook and fill in the missing words in the chart below.

present tense	past tense	past participle
1. break	broke	broken
2. bring	brought	brought
3. come	came	come
4. drink	drank	drunk
5. know	knew	known
6. lead	led	led
7. shake	shook	shaken
8. sing	sang	sung
9. speak	spoke	spoken
10. take	took	taken

The Next Step ● Now open your handbook to page 382 again and check your work. Correct any mistakes you made. Write a sentence using each of the verbs you missed. That will help you remember them next time.

Irregular Verbs 2

The First Step ● This exercise gives you more practice using **irregular verbs.** Before you begin, review the chart of irregular verbs on page 382 of your handbook.

DIRECTIONS: In each sentence below, fill in the blank with the correct form of the verb that's written in parentheses. Try to do it without using your handbook. The first sentence has been done for you as an example.

1. The rain ___*froze*___ and made the streets slick. (freeze)

2. Our cat's water was ___*frozen*___ , too. (freeze)

3. My uncle ___*took*___ me to a museum last week. (take)

4. He has ___*taken*___ me to a lot of fun places. (take)

5. I ___*woke*___ up at 7:00 a.m. yesterday. (wake)

6. I ___*rode*___ my bike to my cousin's house. (ride)

7. I had never ___*ridden*___ there before. (ride)

8. Misha was ___*bitten*___ by a spider. (bite)

9. The spider ___*bit*___ him on the foot. (bite)

10. His neighbor ___*came*___ over to look at it. (come)

11. Misha's mom ___*spoke*___ to the doctor. (speak)

12. The doctor asked if Misha had ___*been*___ going barefoot again. (be)

M·m·m·m·m·m·

The Next Step ● Now check your work. Turn to the chart on page 382, and look up each word that you filled in. Write one sentence for each verb you got wrong. (Use your own paper.)

Verb Tenses

The First Step ● **Verb tenses** tell the time of a verb. (See page 383 of your handbook.)

The **present tense** of a verb describes something that is happening now or something that happens regularly.

Example: The bear **eats**.

The **past tense** of a verb describes something that happened in the past.

Example: The bear **ate**.

The **future tense** of a verb describes something that will happen in the future.

Example: The bear **will eat**.

DIRECTIONS: Circle the present tense verb in each sentence below. Then on the lines after each sentence, write the verb in the past tense and the future tense. (See pages 382 and 383 in your handbook.) The first two sentences have been done for you.

	Past Tense	Future Tense
1. I (play) my stereo at top volume.	played	will play
2. I (sing) along.	sang	will sing
3. But no one (hears) me.	heard	will hear
4. The stereo (is) too loud.	was	will be
5. My brother (goes) nuts.	went	will go
6. My mother (rolls) her eyes.	rolled	will roll
7. My father (laughs).	laughed	will laugh
8. Our dog Elvis (howls).	howled	will howl
9. Our cat Joe Bob (runs) away.	ran	will run
10. But I (have) a good time.	had	will have

Verb Tenses

The Next Step ● List three verbs below. (You can pick three from the list on page 382 of your handbook, or you can use any other verbs.) Have a classmate do the same thing, then trade lists. For each of the three verbs you receive, write three sentences. Use the **present tense** of the verb in one sentence, the **past tense** in another sentence, and the **future tense** in your last sentence.

Three Verbs:

1. _____

2. _____

3. _____

Present tense sentences:

1. _____

2. _____

3. _____

Past tense sentences:

1. _____

2. _____

3. _____

Future tense sentences:

1. _____

2. _____

3. _____

Name

Adjectives

The First Step ● An **adjective** is a word that describes a noun or a pronoun. Sometimes more than one adjective is used to describe a noun or pronoun. (See handbook page 384 for more about adjectives; see topic number 20 on page 346 for information about using commas to separate two or more adjectives.)

Examples:

Realistic fiction is fun to read.

Beverly Cleary writes **funny**, **entertaining** books.

DIRECTIONS: Think about a book of fiction that you have read. See how many adjectives you can come up with that describe the book's characters. Then in the chart below, list the name of the main character, the name of another character, and adjectives to describe each.

Book Title: _____

Adjectives

	(Answers will vary.)	
The Main Character		
One Other Character		

Adjectives

The Next Step ● Now write a descriptive paragraph about one of the characters you have described. Use adjectives from the chart.

_____

_____

_____

_____

_____

_____

_____

_____

_____

_____

_____

_____

_____

_____

_____

Forms of Adjectives

The First Step ● The **positive form** of an adjective describes a noun without comparing it to anyone or anything else. The **comparative form** of an adjective compares two people, places, things, or ideas. And the **superlative form** compares three or more people, places, things, or ideas.

Positive	Miguel is a **fast** runner.
Comparative	He is **faster** than anyone on the team.
Superlative	He is the **fastest** runner in the league.
Positive	Sylvia is a **skillful** skateboarder.
Comparative	She is **more skillful** than she was last year. ("More" is added before an adjective of two or more syllables.)
Superlative	She is now the **most skillful** skateboarder on her block. ("Most" is added before an adjective of two or more syllables.)

DIRECTIONS: Write three sentences about your favorite sport. Use the three forms of an adjective, one in each sentence.

1. _____ *(Answers will vary.)* _____

_____

_____

2. _____

_____

_____

3. _____

_____

_____

Forms of Adjectives

The Next Step ● Write a paragraph about the best or worst experience you have had in sports. You may use some of the sentences you wrote in the first part of this activity. Be sure to use the positive, comparative, and superlative forms of adjectives.

_____

_____

_____

_____

_____

_____

_____

_____

_____

_____

_____

_____

_____

Adverbs

> **The First Step** ● An **adverb** is a word that describes a verb, an adjective, or another adverb. Most adverbs answer when, where, or how questions. (See page 385 in your handbook.)

DIRECTIONS: In the following sentences about field trips, circle the nine adverbs and underline the verbs they describe. The first one is done for you.

Hint: Sometimes more than one adverb in the same sentence can describe the same word.

1. The first-grade class (always) takes a trip to the zoo (early) in the fall.

2. (Sometimes) the second-grade class visits a local farm to pick apples.

3. The third grade (usually) travels (down) to the field museum and then writes a class report about endangered species.

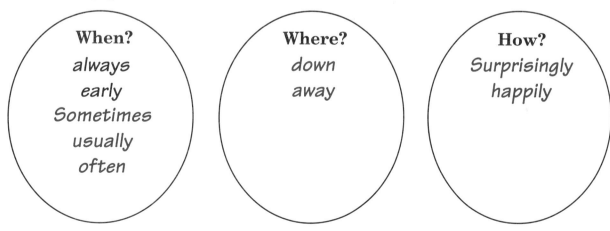

4. (Surprisingly,) the fourth grade (often) votes for a field day to clean up the vacant lots in the neighborhood.

5. The fifth-grade class (happily) goes (away) to camp for three days in the spring.

DIRECTIONS: Now put the adverbs you just found into the circles that answer the following questions for each verb.

When?	**Where?**	**How?**
always	down	Surprisingly
early	away	happily
Sometimes		
usually		
often		

Adverbs

The Next Step ● Sometimes things that weren't planned happen on field trips. Can you remember a surprising incident from a field trip? Write about it. Start your story with the adverb *surprisingly*. Then share your story with your class.

_____

_____

_____

_____

_____

_____

_____

_____

_____

_____

_____

_____

Identifying Prepositional Phrases

The First Step ● A **prepositional phrase** includes a preposition, the object of the preposition, and any describing words that come in between. (See handbook page 386.) The prepositional phrases below describe where the cats are located.

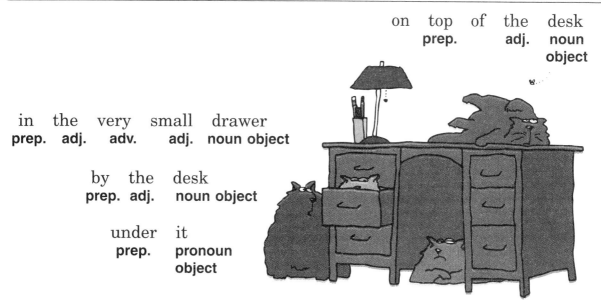

on   top   of   the   desk
prep.   adj.   noun
                          object

in   the   very   small   drawer
prep. adj.   adv.   adj.   noun object

by   the   desk
prep. adj.   noun object

under   it
prep.   pronoun
         object

DIRECTIONS: Write a prepositional phrase next to each balloon in this picture. Each phrase should tell where that balloon is located. Label the prepositions and noun objects in the phrases. (See page 386 in your handbook.)

(Answers will vary.)

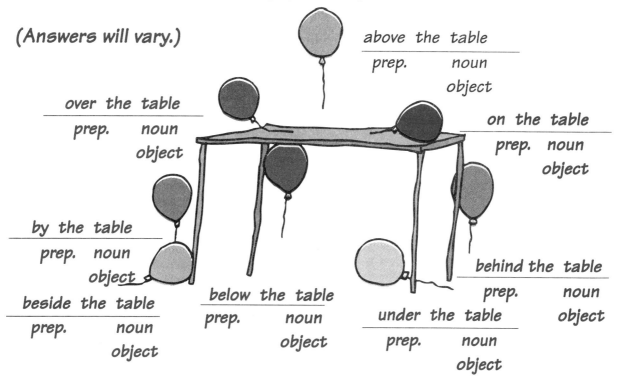

above the table
prep.   noun
             object

over the table
prep.   noun
         object

on the table
prep. noun
         object

by the table
prep. noun
       object

below the table
prep.   noun
           object

behind the table
prep.   noun
           object

under the table
prep.   noun
           object

beside the table
prep.   noun
           object

Understanding Our Language **101**

Prepositional Phrases

The First Step ● A **prepositional phrase** includes a preposition, the object of the preposition, and any describing words that come in between. (See handbook page 386 for a list of prepositions.)

DIRECTIONS: Write as many prepositional phrases as you can about this picture. We think you can write at least 10; we've written the first one for you.

1. *behind the tiny mouse*

2. _____ *(Answers will vary.)* _____

3. _____

4. _____

5. _____

6. _____

7. _____

8. _____

9. _____

10. _____

11. _____

12. _____

13. _____

14. _____

Interjections

> **The First Step** ● An **interjection** is a word or phrase used to express strong emotion or surprise. A comma or an exclamation point is used to separate an interjection from the rest of the sentence. (See page 387 in your handbook.)

Examples:

Yikes! The cat's in the top tree branches!

Wow! Did you see that Harley?

Hey! Watch where you're going!

Man, that's dangerous!

Oh, no! I think she's going to fall!

DIRECTIONS: Pretend you are talking on the phone to your friend. At the same time, you're looking out the window and see something very surprising. Choose one of the sentences above as a starting point for writing a story. Tell your friend about what you are observing. Use a variety of interjections and short sentences to describe what you "see" from the window.

(Answers will vary.)

Using Conjunctions

> **The First Step** ● **Conjunctions** are connecting words. The three kinds of conjunctions are explained on page 387 of your handbook.

DIRECTIONS: Use conjunctions to connect the following sentences. You may have to make some changes in wording to make your new sentence read smoothly and correctly. The kind of conjunction you should use is written in parentheses. See pages 93 and 387 in the handbook for more about using conjunctions.)

(Answers may vary.)

1. Robby went to class. Robby went to lunch. (coordinate conjunction)

   Robby went to class and to lunch.

2. I worked on my homework. I didn't finish it. (coordinate conjunction)

   I worked on my homework, but I didn't finish it.

3. It was raining. The game was canceled. (coordinate conjunction)

   It was raining, so the game was canceled.

4. I made my lunch. I went to school. (subordinate conjunction)

   I made my lunch before I went to school.

5. We stopped playing. It started raining. (subordinate conjunction)

   We stopped playing when it started raining.

6. We went to get pizza. The game was canceled. (subordinate conjunction)

   We went to get pizza after the game was canceled.

7. Our team didn't want to play. The other team didn't want to play. (correlative conjunction)

   Neither our team nor the other team wanted to play.

8. The game was canceled. We'll have to make it up. (coordinate conjunction)

   The game was canceled, so we'll have to make it up.

Minilessons
Answer Key

The minilessons in this section cover basic editing and proofreading skills. All the minilessons are cross-referenced with the handbook.

Marking Punctuation Minilessons

Short Change . . . . *Periods*

LIST three different ways periods are used in the following sentences besides as the end punctuation of each sentence (topic number 01). Then CHECK your handbook (**pages 343-344**) to see how you did.

1. I might as well change my name to I. M. Short.
2. I only have $4.93, and I owe my neighbor $5.75.
3. When I tell her my problem, I'm sure that Ms. Jackson will not be very happy.

1. *I.M.—after an initial (topic number 03)*

2. *$4.93, $5.75—as a decimal (topic number 04)*

3. *Ms.—after abbreviations (topic number 05)*

What's that comma doing there? . . . . *Commas*

TURN to **page 150** of your handbook. See the model report "The Big Chill" by Todd Michael? There are eight commas in the report. On the lines below, WRITE down the rule that explains why each comma is there. (You'll find all the rules for using commas under topic numbers on **pages 345** and **346** in your handbook.) The first rule has been written in for you. (Work on this with a partner.)

1. *parade,—to set off long phrases and clauses (topic number 23)*

2. *lap,—to set off long phrases and clauses (topic number 23)*

3. *on,—between two independent clauses (topic number 16)*

4. *say,—to set off dialogue (topic number 17)*

5. *Mom,—in direct address (topic number 18)*

6. *says,—to set off dialogue (topic number 17)*

7. *Charlotte,—between two independent clauses (topic number 16)*

8. *say,—to set off dialogue (topic number 17)*

Dates & Addresses . . . . *Commas*

PUT commas where they belong in the dates and addresses below. For help, see topic number 13 on **page 345** in your handbook.

1. On January 15, 1986, Martin Luther King's birthday became a legal holiday.

2. On February 12, 1866, Lincoln's birthday was first observed as a holiday.

3. The Fourth of July was first celebrated in Philadelphia on July 4, 1777.

4. My address is   *212 N. Spring Street, Wildrose, IL 60201.*

(Answers will vary.)

(Fill in the blank.)

The frog caught the fly—ZAP! . . . . *Dashes*

To each of the following sentences, ADD the word or phrase that appears next to it. Set off the added words with dashes. (Remember, dashes show a quick change in direction or an interruption in the flow of thought.) An example has been done for you. Also see **page 348** of your handbook.

(Answers will vary.)

1. A frog landed right in my lap.   **plop!**

   A frog landed—plop!—right in my lap.

2. My little sister jumped out the window.   **she was born goofy**

   My little sister—she was born goofy—jumped out the window.

3. I finished my homework and went to bed.   **at last**

   I finished my homework—at last—and went to bed.

4. The alarm clock went off at 6:00 a.m.   **RINGGG!!!**

   The alarm clock—RINGGG!!!—went off at 6:00 a.m.

5. She slammed the door and yelled at me.   **BANG!**

   She slammed the door—BANG!—and yelled at me.

6. School will be out for the summer in three days.   **hooray!**

   School will be out for the summer—hooray!—in three days.

What's does it mean? . . . . *Apostrophes*

WRITE the word or phrase that each of the following contractions represents. CHECK your work by looking up each contraction in the dictionary. Then, on your own paper, USE the contractions in sentences. You may use more than one contraction in each sentence. Also see **page 349** in your handbook.

1. I'll	*I will*	4. we'd	*we would*
2. it's	*it is*	5. they're	*they are*
3. doesn't	*does not*	6. haven't	*have not*

Information, Please . . . . *Parentheses*

To each of the following sentences, ADD the word or phrase that appears next to it. Set off the added words with parentheses. (Remember, parentheses set off words that add information or make something clearer.) Two examples have been done for you. Also see **page 351** in your handbook.

1. My brothers are in the second grade.   **they're twins**

   My brothers (they're twins) are in the second grade.

2. I have three cats.   **two tabbies and one gray tiger**

   I have three cats (two tabbies and one gray tiger).

3. My grandmother has a garden.   **my mother's mother**

   My grandmother (my mother's mother) has a garden.

4. My grandfather likes to play tennis.   **he's 63!**

   My gandfather (he's 63!) likes to play tennis.

5. I have two watches.   **a green one and a black one**

   I have two watches (a green one and a black one).

6. My brother plays the guitar.   **the one who's in high school**

   My brother (the one who's in high school) plays the guitar.

Editing for Mechanics Minilessons

Give me an example. *Capitalization*

Pages 352-354 of your handbook list the rules for capitalization. The rules are found under topic numbers 63-76. FIND each of the topic numbers listed below. READ each rule. Then, on the line next to each topic number, WRITE one example of a word or phrase that is capitalized according to the rule. Do not write a word that is shown in your handbook. The first example has been done for you. THINK of the rest on your own!

65. *Grandpa*   74. _____

67.   *(Answers will vary.)*   75. _____

72. _____   76. _____

What if there's more than one? . . . . *Plurals*

WRITE the plural forms of the following words. Then, LOOK UP the words in a dictionary to check your work. See **page 355** of your handbook for help.

1. box   *boxes*
2. puppy   *puppies*
3. cookie   *cookies*
4. tree   *trees*
5. candy   *candies*

6. cloud   *clouds*
7. monkey   *monkeys*
8. lunch   *lunches*
9. roof   *roofs*
10. radio   *radios*

Two Ways to Write Numbers . . . . *Numbers*

FILL IN the blanks in the following sentences. WRITE either "numerals" or "words," whichever is correct. See **page 356** in your handbook for help.

1. When numbers appear at the beginning of a sentence, they are always written as ____**words**____ .

2. Numbers less than 10 are usually written as ____**words**____ .

3. Numbers greater than 10 are usually written as ____**numerals**____ .

4. Numbers are written as ____**numerals**____ when they are in dates, times, and addresses.

5. Numbers that are amounts of money are written as ____**numerals**____ .

Taking Shortcuts . . . . *Abbreviations*

MATCH each of the following abbreviations to the word or phrase it represents. See **pages 356** and **357** in your handbook for help.

h 1. Mr.   a. et cetera (and so forth)

f 2. Mrs.   b. as soon as possible

e 3. Ms.   c. kilogram

a 4. etc.   d. post meridiem (after noon)

g 5. a.m.   e. polite form of address for a woman

d 6. p.m.   f. Missus

b 7. ASAP   g. ante meridiem (before noon)

c 8. kg   h. Mister

Checking Your Spelling Minilessons

ATTENTION! . . . . *Check Your Spelling*

Words get special attention by being capitalized. Some words are *always* capitalized!

LIST at least 10 capitalized words from the list of frequently misspelled words on **pages 358-361** in your handbook.

WRITE each one in the column under the rule it fits.

People	Days, Holidays	Months	Nationalities
Santa Claus	Christmas,	April, August,	American
	Easter, Friday,	December,	
	Monday, Saturday,	February, January,	
	Sunday,	July, June, March,	
	Thanksgiving,	May, November,	
	Thursday, Tuesday,	October,	
	and Wednesday	and September	

"C" Snakes . . . . *Check Your Spelling*

Certain words appear in the list of commonly misspelled words on **pages 358-361** in your handbook because they have letters that are pronounced like other letters. "Certain" is one of those words. The "c" makes the sound of "s." It sounds like the word should be spelled "sertain."

LIST at least 10 other words in which a "c" makes the "s" sound on **pages 358-361** in your handbook. The first word has been listed for you.

1. *accept*
2. *accident*
3. *century*
4. *city*
5. *audience*
6. *bicycle*
7. *celebration*
8. *cemetery*
9. *patience*
10. *(Answers will vary.)*

Using the Right Word Minilessons

On the Board . . . . *Usage: "A" or "An"?*

FILL IN the blanks in the sentences below, using "a" or "an," whichever is correct. Check **page 362** in your handbook for help.

1. Our classroom has ___*a*___ bulletin board.

2. There is ___*a*___ calendar on the board.

3. Once ___*a*___ month, we put new pictures on the board.

4. Right now, there are pictures of ___*an*___ eagle, ___*an*___ owl, and

___*a*___ parrot on the board.

5. Paula has ___*an*___ idea for next month's board.

6. She wants to put up pictures of ___*an*___ astronaut.

A Pet Named Dino . . . . *Usage: "Its" or "It's"?*

FILL IN the blanks in the sentences below, using "its" or "it's," whichever is correct. Check **page 365** in your handbook for help.

I have a pet lizard. ___*Its*___ name is Dino, and ___*it's*___ green and

shiny. ___*Its*___ home is an aquarium. ___*Its*___ favorite food is flies.

Dino thinks ___*it's*___ fun to sneak out of the aquarium and explore my

room. But ___*it's*___ not so fun when the cat comes around. ___*It's*___ a good

thing for Dino that a lizard can "drop" ___*its*___ tail in an emergency. Last

week the cat put ___*its*___ paw on Dino's tail. My pet lizard lost ___*its*___ tail,

but ___*it's*___ growing back already.

You're your own best friend. . . . . *Usage: "Your" or "You're"?*

FILL IN the blanks in the sentences below, using "your" or "you're," whichever is correct. Check **page 369** in your handbook for help.

1. Is Paula _____*your*_____ sister?

2. _____*You're*_____ Paula's brother, aren't you?

3. _____*You're*_____ as tall as Sabrina.

4. Sabrina is _____*your*_____ height.

5. Is Carlos in _____*your*_____ class?

6. _____*You're*_____ in the same class as Carlos, aren't you?

7. _____*You're*_____ a lot younger than _____*your*_____
   teacher.

8. _____*Your*_____ teacher said _____*you're*_____ a lot younger than
   he is.

Understanding Sentences Minilessons

Fair Game . . . . *Kinds of Sentences*

PRETEND you're at a carnival or a fair, standing near the wild rides and in
view of the fireworks display. People all around you are talking.

WRITE two declarative sentences, two interrogative sentences, two imperative
sentences, and two exclamatory sentences that you might hear from the
crowd. For more information on the kinds of sentences see **page 373** in
your handbook. Here are some sample sentences to get you started. Write
your sentences on your own paper.

Declarative:
I rode the Zipper 10 times in a row.

Interrogative:
How many goldfish did you win?

Imperative:
Don't eat too much cotton candy.

Exclamatory:
That's awesome!

Filling In Fragments . . . . *Sentence Fragments*

CHOOSE two paragraphs from one of your favorite books or stories.

TURN the sentences in the paragraphs into sentence fragments. (See **page 87**
in your handbook for an explanation of fragments.) Make sure some of
your fragments need subjects, and some need verbs.

TRADE with a partner and CORRECT each other's fragments by making them
into complete sentences.

Finally, COMPARE your corrected sentences with the original sentences.
Remember, they don't have to be exactly the same as long as they're
correct.

Getting to Know You . . . . *Sentence Fragments*

WRITE sentence fragments that give facts about people in your class. Write
three fragments that need a verb. (Example: Last summer, Jackie) Write
three fragments that need a subject. (Example: takes clarinet lessons)

TRADE with a classmate. Try to turn each other's fragments into correct,
complete sentences. You'll find out how well you know your classmates!

The pig crashed into the cow. .... *Run-On Sentences*

WRITE three run-on sentences that are all about things running into each other. (**Example:** My dad backed our car into our neighbor's car the two cars locked bumpers.)

EXCHANGE your run-on sentences and CORRECT them. If you need help, see **page 87** in your handbook.

Scrambling Sentences .... *Run-On Sentences*

CHOOSE two or three paragraphs from one of your favorite books or stories.

TURN most of the sentences in the paragraphs into run-on sentences. (See **page 87** in your handbook for an explanation of run-ons.) TRADE with a partner and CORRECT each other's sentences.

Finally, COMPARE your corrected sentences with the original sentences. Yours don't have to be exactly the same, as long as they're correct.

And Then I Said .... *Rambling Sentences*

WRITE a rambling sentence about how you spent one day. It could be a day at school, at an amusement park, or anywhere. (**Page 87** in your handbook gives an example of a rambling sentence.) Include what you did, what you ate, how you felt, and so on. When you're done, go back and CORRECT your rambling sentence. Make your new sentences as smooth and as fun to read as possible.

READ the five pairs of sentences below. For each pair of sentences, DECIDE whether you would use a compound subject or a compound verb to combine the two sentences into one. WRITE "subject" or "verb" on the line next to the sentences. Then COMBINE the sentences on the lines below. Use **page 92** in your handbook to help you.

(Answers will vary.)

1. Jupiter is bigger than Mercury.
   Saturn is bigger than Mercury. _____ *subject* _____

   Jupiter and Saturn are bigger than Mercury.

   _____

2. Pluto is small.
   Pluto takes 247 years to orbit the sun. _____ *verb* _____

   Pluto is small and takes 247 years to orbit the sun.

   _____

3. Pluto is far away from the sun.
   Neptune is far away from the sun. _____ *subject* _____

   Pluto and Neptune are far away from the sun.

   _____

4. Saturn has rings.
   Saturn is cold. _____ *verb* _____

   Saturn is cold and has rings.

   _____

5. Mercury has no moons.
   Venus has no moons. _____ *subject* _____

   Mercury and Venus have no moons.

   _____

Name That State . . . . *Combining Sentences*

FILL IN the blanks in the sentences below. Use the map on **page 405** of your handbook to help you. Then COMBINE each set of sentences into one sentence. (See **page 91** in your handbook.) An example has been done for you.

Virginia is on the Atlantic Ocean.

1. _____North Carolina_____ is on the Atlantic Ocean.

2. _____Georgia_____ is on the Atlantic Ocean.

3. _Virginia, North Carolina, and Georgia are on the Atlantic Ocean._

California is on the Pacific Ocean.

4. ___(Answers will vary.)___ is on the Pacific Ocean.

5. _____ is on the Pacific Ocean.

6. _____

Mississippi is a southern state.

7. _____ is a southern state.

8. _____ is a southern state.

9. _____

Arizona is a western state.

10. _____ is a western state.

11. _____ is a western state.

12. _____

Texas is on the border of Mexico.

13. _____ is on the border of Mexico.

14. _____ is on the border of Mexico.

15. _____

Understanding Our Language Minilessons

Noun Sense . . . . *Kinds of Nouns*

STUDY the chart of common and proper nouns on **page 375** in your
handbook. NOTE how a specific proper noun is listed for each common
noun. Of course, there could be many proper nouns for any of the common
nouns. For example, you could have different mountains—the Alps, the
White Mountains, and so on.

LIST as many more examples of common nouns and matching proper nouns as
you can in 5 minutes.

Then CHOOSE your favorite pair of common and proper nouns. WRITE the
most interesting sentence you can, using the common noun.

Example:

The year after I hiked up a <u>peak</u>, it was declared too dangerous

to climb without ropes.

Then REWRITE the sentence substituting the proper noun for the common
noun. (Notice how specific proper nouns can improve your writing.)

Example:

The year after I hiked up <u>Buckskin Mountain</u>, it was declared

too dangerous to climb without ropes.

School Fun . . . . *Using Nouns*

THINK about a recent time when you had fun at school. It could be during a classroom project, lunchtime, recess, or a special program or sports event. LIST various nouns that might be used when writing or talking about your experience.

Then WRITE a paragraph about the experience, using nouns from your list. SHARE your paragraph with the class.

They agree! . . . . *Agreement of Pronouns*

STUDY "Agreement of Pronouns" on the top of **page 378** in your handbook. Notice that the word "antecedent" refers to the noun that the pronoun replaces. Antecedent means "comes before." A pronoun must *always* have a noun that comes before it.

SPEND several minutes writing a list of interesting nouns. SELECT your favorite noun from the list. Then WRITE a sentence using that noun and also a pronoun that refers back to it.

SHARE your sentence with the class. Decide whether the pronouns in each sentence agree with the nouns they replace.

I second that. . . . . *Person of a Pronoun*

STUDY "Person of a Pronoun" on **page 378** in your handbook. Then TURN to "Start the Story" on **page 157**. Notice the third-person pronouns in the two paragraphs about Cynthia.

CROSS OUT the *third*-person pronouns and replace them with *first*-person pronouns. The noun (Cynthia) has been changed for you.

> *I*
> ~~Cynthia~~ had no warning. One minute there ~~she~~ *I* was, floating on
> *My*
> soft pillows of warm air. ~~Her~~ wings were stretched wide while ~~she~~ *I*
> *my*
> admired ~~her~~ neighborhood. Here and there among the trees a
> *me*
> swimming pool glinted at ~~her~~, a miniature car winked in the sun, and
>
> tiny people followed sidewalks, never thinking to look up to see
> *me*
> ~~Cynthia Bean~~ gliding over their heads.

Now, CROSS OUT the *third*-person pronouns and replace them with *second*-person pronouns. Change a verb to agree with a pronoun if necessary. The noun (Cynthia) has been changed for you.

> *You*   *you were*
> ~~Cynthia~~ had no warning. One minute there she ~~was~~, floating on
> *Your*   *you*
> soft pillows of warm air. ~~Her~~ wings were stretched wide while ~~she~~
> *your*
> admired ~~her~~ neighborhood. Here and there among the trees a
> *you*
> swimming pool glinted at ~~her~~, a miniature car winked in the sun, and
>
> tiny people followed sidewalks, never thinking to look up to see
> *you*
> ~~Cynthia Bean~~ gliding over their heads.

COMPARE the three versions. With a partner, talk about the advantages and disadvantages of each.

122 *Understanding Our Language Minilessons*

Points of View . . . . *Person of a Pronoun*

STUDY the section "Person of a Pronoun" on **page 378** in your handbook.
   Then, on **page 82,** find and read the story "I'm Growing Up."
Working with a partner, have one person READ the selection, changing all the
   first-person references to *second-person* pronouns. (Make the changes as you
   read out loud, but quietly, to your partner.) Then have the other person
   READ the same selection, changing all the *first-person* references to *third-
   person* pronouns.
DISCUSS the effect of changing the point of view in reading or writing a story.
   SHARE your findings with a classmate.

Who's talking? . . . . *Person of a Pronoun*

Using the discussion about the person of a pronoun on **page 378** in your
   handbook, PRACTICE identifying the point of view of various writings.
   LOOK at **pages 115** and **125** in your handbook, and IDENTIFY the point
   of view for each of these student models to get you started.

1. When I Got Burned . . .   _____*first person*_____

2. JAWS!   _____*third person*_____

Special Challenge: IDENTIFY the author's point of view in your free-reading
   books, other school texts, and even newspaper and magazine stories.

It just don't sound right! . . . . . . *Singular and Plural Verbs*

LOOK at the top of **page 381** in your handbook. Then ANSWER the

questions: What's wrong with the title of this minilesson? *The subject*

"it" and the verb "don't" do not agree.

What should the sentence be? *It just doesn't sound right!*

Now WRITE two sentences—one that uses a subject and verb that *agree,* and
   one that uses a subject and verb that *do not agree.* Without saying which
   one you are reading, READ one of your sentences to a partner. Do you both
   agree? Do the subject and the verb in your sentence agree or not?
Note: You will probably know whether the subject and verb agree if they
   sound right. You naturally know a great deal about your language already.

Move over, ED. . . . . *Irregular Verbs*

FILL IN the correct forms of the verbs in the sentence patterns below. USE
these verbs: call, eat, walk, run, swim, play, learn, go, sit.

Example:

1. Now I ___call___ . Earlier I ___called___ . In the past I have ___called___ .

2. Now I ___eat___ . Earlier I ___ate___ . In the past I have ___eaten___ .

3. Now I ___walk___ . Earlier I ___walked___ . In the past I have ___walked___ .

4. Now I ___run___ . Earlier I ___ran___ . In the past I have ___run___ .

5. Now I ___swim___ . Earlier I ___swam___ . In the past I have ___swum___ .

6. Now I ___play___ . Earlier I ___played___ . In the past I have ___played___ .

7. Now I ___learn___ . Earlier I ___learned___ . In the past I have ___learned___ .

8. Now I ___go___ . Earlier I ___went___ . In the past I have ___gone___ .

9. Now I ___sit___ . Earlier I ___sat___ . In the past I have ___sat___ .

LOOK at the list of words you have written. Are there any ending patterns
that are the same? Are some of the endings very different?

TURN to "Irregular Verbs" on **pages 381-382** in your handbook. Check your
endings. Refer to the chart on **page 382** whenever you have questions
about irregular verbs in your writing.

Cut-and-Paste . . . . *Adjectives*

FIND pictures of nouns. Using magazines, old catalogs, or ads, find one
picture that shows a *person,* a second that shows a *place,* and a third that
shows a *thing*.

CUT out the three pictures and MOUNT each at the top of a sheet of paper.
Below each picture, LIST as many words as you can to describe that picture.
See **page 384** in your handbook for more information about adjectives. Then
WRITE one sentence at the bottom of each page using your best adjectives.

Special Challenge: SHARE your pictures, lists, and sentences with the class.
You may do this by giving brief oral reports or by selecting your best
picture and sentence for a bulletin-board display.

The Four Seasons . . . . *Adjectives*

WRITE an acrostic (name) poem for one of the four seasons—winter, spring, summer, autumn. USE only adjectives. See **page 384** in your handbook for more about adjectives; see "Name Poetry" on **page 187** for more about an acrostic poem.

Example:

> **WINTER**
> **W**hite
> **I**cy
> **N**asty
> **T**errific
> **E**ndless
> **R**adiant

Then CREATE a four-seasons bulletin board, decorated with original artwork.

Special Challenge: THINK of other themes for writing acrostic poems—the four directions on the compass, the colors of the rainbow, and so on. Consider themes that would make dramatic bulletin boards for sharing your poems.

Go fish! . . . . *Adverbs*

SEE "Adverb" on **page 385** in your handbook to see how adverbs add meaning to verbs. Then CHOOSE words from the list below, and WRITE at least five sentences on your paper. Each sentence should have five words or more.

swam	ran	fast	Tim	I
after	quickly	jogged	slowly	park
road	party	backyard	pool	Bev
with	to	friends	her	angrily
his	my	school	home	often
from	the	in	and	it

After you write your sentences, LABEL the nouns (N), verbs (V), and adverbs (A) in each of your sentences.

Example:

Bev and I ran quickly to the park.
  N   V   A   N

When, Where, How . . . . *Adverbs*

READ about how adverbs are used on **page 385** in your handbook.

DRAW a picture of one of your favorite activities. Show lots of action! Then WRITE three sentences about your drawing that include strong action verbs. USE adverbs, also, to answer *when, where,* and *how*—one question for each sentence.

SEE the examples at the top of **page 385**.

Find Festus! . . . . *Prepositions*

READ about prepositions and prepositional phrases on **page 386** in your handbook. Then TURN to **page 111** in your handbook and READ "The Great Gerbil Escape." FIND and WRITE down the prepositional phrases from the first four paragraphs in this story.

LABEL the part of speech of each object of the preposition in your phrases. The first one has been done for you.

Paragraph 1:
noun   *noun*
of gerbils, from our bathtub

Paragraph 2:
noun
in your tub

Paragraph 3:
noun   *noun*
over the edge, of the tub

Paragraph 4:
noun   *noun*   *noun*
down the heat vent, in the wall, beside the vent,
noun   *noun*
into the vent, in a towel

Making Connections . . . . *Conjunctions*

READ the definition of a conjunction on **page 387** in your handbook. The
most common conjunctions are: **and, because, but, or,** and **so**.

READ the story "The Unforgettable Autograph" on **page 81** in your handbook.
See if you can FIND all the conjunctions in the story. NOTICE how they
connect words and groups of words.

1.	*because*	5.	*and*	
2.	*while*	6.	*while*	
3.	*and*	7.	*but*	
4.	*and*			

Then LOOK for conjunctions in something you have written.

Categories . . . . *Parts of Speech Overview*

CREATE a table with five spaces across and five spaces down. WRITE five
letters down the side and five names of the parts of speech across the top.
(One possibility has been provided below.) FILL IN the table with as many
words as you can.

THINK of ways that you could turn this activity into a game (like tic-tac-toe or
bingo).

(Answers will vary.)

	noun	adverb	preposition	verb	adjective
m	**muskrat**	**more**	—	**make**	**mad**
b					
f					
w					
a					

Check-It-Out Daily Sentences Answer Key

The Check-It-Out Daily Sentences in this section of the SourceBook come in two different varieties. The focused sentences help students concentrate on one proofreading skill at a time. The proofreading sentences provide two or three different types of errors for students to correct.

Focused Sentences

● **End Punctuation**

What you actually see in a mirror is the light bouncing back to show a reverse image of the real object **.**

● **End Punctuation**

Did you know that California was named after a character in a popular Spanish novel **?**

● **End Punctuation**

Wake up, America—hula hoops are back **!**

● **End Punctuation**

Always be careful about proofreading your writing assignments **.**

● **End Punctuation**

An African elephant could flap up a strong breeze with those ears, wouldn't you agree **?**

Focused Sentences

● **Commas (In a Series)**

The U.S. team at the first Olympics in 1896 consisted of seven runners⹁ a pole-vaulter⹁ a shot-putter⹁ and a hurdler.

● **Commas (In a Series)**

On Saturday mornings I watch cartoons⹁ eat breakfast⹁ help clean the house⹁ and wash the dog.

● **Commas (In a Series)**

Here's a list of my least favorite vegetables: broccoli⹁ lima beans⹁ cauliflower⹁ beets⹁ and artichokes.

● **Commas (In a Series)**

My favorite cars are the 1965 Ford Mustang⹁ the 1957 Chevy⹁ and the Volkswagon Beetle.

● **Commas (In a Series)**

Anteaters have eyes⹁ ears⹁ noses⹁ and mouths, but no teeth.

Focused Sentences

● **Commas (In Dates and Addresses)**

Valentina V. Tereshkova of the U.S.S.R. was the first
woman to travel in outer space on June 16, 1963.

● **Commas (In Dates and Addresses)**

Animal lovers may join Ranger Rick's Nature Club, 8925
Leesburg Pike, Vienna, Virginia 22184.

● **Commas (In Dates and Addresses)**

On May 30, 1959, Wilt Chamberlain began playing for the
Philadelphia Warriors.

● **Commas (In Dates and Addresses)**

May Day first became a day to honor workers on
May 1, 1890, in England.

● **Commas (In Dates and Addresses)**

On January 20, 1993, President Clinton and his family moved
to 1600 Pennsylvania Avenue, Washington, D.C.

Focused Sentences

● **Commas (Between Independent Clauses)**

Most fish do not sleep ⌄ but some types actually stand
on their tails and lean against coral for a snooze.

● **Commas (Between Independent Clauses)**

You'd expect a centipede to have a hundred legs ⌄ but sometimes
it has more than a hundred legs.

● **Commas (Between Independent Clauses)**

The Ford family adopted young Leslie and changed his name to
Gerald ⌄ but they couldn't have known he would one day be
President Ford.

● **Commas (Between Independent Clauses)**

President Andrew Jackson was born in South Carolina ⌄ and he
became the first man born in a log cabin to be elected
president of the United States.

● **Commas (Between Independent Clauses)**

Quicksand can suck animals down to their deaths ⌄ but a person
can escape by lying flat and rolling out.

Focused Sentences

● **Commas (To Set Off Appositives)**

Lotto‸ a game first played in Europe‸ is called bingo in America.

● **Commas (To Set Off Appositives)**

The metric system‸ a system based on 10‸ does not have fractions as we know them.

● **Commas (To Set Off Appositives)**

Paper bags‸ the kind groceries come in‸ are excellent hiding places for cats.

● **Commas (To Set Off Appositives)**

The staff of Aesculapius‸ the Greek god of medicine‸ is used as an ambulance symbol.

● **Commas (To Set Off Appositives)**

The outer bark of a tree‸ the rhytidome‸ protects the tender inner bark.

Focused Sentences

● **Commas (To Set Off Long Phrases and Clauses)**

If you ever travel on a boat or ship, you should know that the left side is called the port while the right side is called the starboard.

● **Commas (To Set Off Long Phrases and Clauses)**

For a ship to travel safely at night, the left side carries a red light while the right side has a green light.

● **Commas (To Set Off Long Phrases and Clauses)**

Before the Berlin Wall came down, Germany was divided into East Germany and West Germany.

● **Commas (To Set Off Long Phrases and Clauses)**

Because of the growing hole in the ozone layer, the Environmental Protection Agency issued stricter pollution guidelines in 1991.

● **Commas (To Set Off Long Phrases and Clauses)**

Three years after Boy's Life magazine was published, American Girl was introduced.

Focused Sentences

● **Semicolon**

Watching videos is fun; however, there's something special about seeing movies on a big screen in a darkened theater.

● **Semicolon**

Mirrors reflect your image; a pool of still water can do the same thing.

● **Semicolon**

Magnifying glasses make small things look larger; some people use them to read tiny print or look at ants.

● **Semicolon**

December 31, 1999, should be a historic New Year's Eve; the next day will be January 1, 2000.

● **Semicolon**

We go to our state fair to see the animals; however, we also enjoy the cream puffs, cotton candy, and corn on the cob.

Focused Sentences

● **Hyphen**

Well ⁀informed football fans know that the Green Bay

Packers beat the Kansas City Chiefs in the first Super Bowl.

● **Hyphen**

My great ⁀aunt had 18 children; one ⁀half were boys and the

other half were girls.

● **Hyphen**

The Beatles, a well ⁀known musical group, released 29 records

in 1964.

● **Hyphen**

The highest ⁀scoring basketball game ever occurred in 1983 when

the Detroit Pistons outscored the Denver Nuggets, 186-183.

● **Hyphen**

I would guess that two ⁀thirds of the class knows that you

cannot divide a one ⁀syllable word at the end of a line.

138 *Check-It-Out Daily Sentences*

Focused Sentences

● **Apostrophes**

Although it ~~isnt~~ *isn't* a popular critter, a ~~fleas~~ *flea's* remarkable

strength allows it to jump 200 times its length.

● **Apostrophes**

Koala ~~bears~~ *bears'* main food is eucalyptus leaves.

● **Apostrophes**

Alexander Graham ~~Bells~~ *Bell's* first telephone was displayed in

~~Philadelphias~~ *Philadelphia's* Exhibition Hall in 1876.

● **Apostrophes**

Harriet Beecher ~~Stowes~~ *Stowe's* book Uncle ~~Toms~~ *Tom's* Cabin made people

aware of the evils of slavery.

● **Apostrophes**

Charles ~~Dickens~~ *Dickens'* books tell about his concern for the poor

people of his day.

Focused Sentences

● **Quotation Marks**

When astronaut Neil Armstrong stepped onto the moon,
he said, "That's one small step for man; one giant leap
for mankind."

● **Quotation Marks**

The skydiving instructor asked, "Who wants to go first?"

● **Quotation Marks**

The expression "yo" has been around for nearly 400 years.

● **Quotation Marks**

The word "run" has dozens of meanings in the dictionary.

● **Quotation Marks**

I always laugh when I read Shel Silverstein's poem
"Jumping Rope."

Focused Sentences

● **Capitalization**

The empire state building in new york city is not as
tall as the sears tower in chicago, illinois.

(corrections shown above words: E empire, S state, B building, N new, Y york, C city, S sears, T tower, C chicago, I illinois)

● **Capitalization**

The people christopher columbus called indians, today like to
be called native americans.

(corrections: C christopher, C columbus, I indians, N native, A americans)

● **Capitalization**

jan e. matzeliger made the first shoe-stitching machine in
america.

(corrections: J jan, E e., M matzeliger, A america)

● **Capitalization**

I learned from mom that president clinton is from hope,
arkansas.

(corrections: M mom, P president, C clinton, H hope, A arkansas)

● **Capitalization**

Did you know that cuba is the largest country in the
caribbean sea?

(corrections: C cuba, C caribbean, S sea)

Focused Sentences

● **Plurals**

We grabbed our ~~paintes~~ *paints* and ~~brushs~~ *brushes* and headed for the

art room.

● **Plurals**

My mother uses her sharpest ~~knifes~~ *knives* to cut the ~~loafs~~ *loaves* of bread.

● **Plurals**

Pianos
~~Pianoes~~ are popular because they can produce a wide range

sounds
of ~~soundes~~.

● **Plurals**

My little brother enjoys chasing ~~bunnys~~ *bunnies* and ~~gooses~~ *geese* at the park.

● **Plurals**

For supper Mom prepared two ~~platesful~~ *platefuls* of ~~tacoes~~ *tacos* and burritos.

Focused Sentences

CHECK IT OUT

● Numbers

64 million
The Pacific Ocean covers ~~64,000,000~~ square miles.

● Numbers

1994
In the year ~~nineteen hundred and ninety-four,~~ almost

60
~~sixty~~ percent of the world's people lived in Asia.

● Numbers

2025
By the year ~~two thousand and twenty-five,~~ experts think

the population in the United States will be about

300
~~three hundred~~ million.

● Numbers

Ten   *4*
~~10~~ students are supposed to report on chapter ~~four~~ while

the other 11 report on chapter 5.

● Numbers

11:00 (or 11 a.m.)   *11*
At ~~eleven~~ a.m. on November ~~eleven,~~ 1919, the peace

agreement ending World War I was signed.

Focused Sentences

● **Using the Right Word**

There   no   wear
~~Their~~ is ~~know~~ real reason why painters ~~where~~ white, but

                  do
they almost always ~~due~~.

● **Using the Right Word**

         their   to hear your
Dogs tilt ~~there~~ heads to the side ~~too~~ ~~here~~ ~~you're~~ voice.

● **Using the Right Word**

Principals   principles
~~Principles~~ are people with strong ~~principals~~.

● **Using the Right Word**

Our   to teach   hole
~~Hour~~ science teacher is going ~~two~~ ~~learn~~ us about the ~~whole~~ in

the ozone layer.

● **Using the Right Word**

Some stationery seems   to write
~~Sum~~ ~~stationary~~ ~~seams~~ too pretty ~~too~~ ~~right~~ on.

Focused Sentences

(Answers may vary.)

● **Combining Sentences**

Math was very hard yesterday. Math was very hard today.
I'm going to ask for special help.

Math was very hard yesterday and today, so I'm going to ask for special help.

● **Combining Sentences**

Earth orbits our sun. Eight other planets orbit our sun.

Earth and eight other planets orbit our sun.

● **Combining Sentences**

Everyone likes cute, furry animals.
Naturalists even like spiders and insects.

Everyone likes cute, furry animals, but naturalists even like spiders and insects.

● **Combining Sentences**

One American mile equals 5,280 feet.
One American mile equals 1,609.3 meters.

One American mile equals 5,280 feet or 1,609.3 meters.

● **Combining Sentences**

Lobsters are red. Lobsters run backward.
Lobsters taste good when cooked and buttered.

Lobsters are red, run backward, and taste good when cooked and buttered.

Focused Sentences

- **Subject-Verb Agreement**

  are
  Cirrus clouds ~~is~~ the highest clouds in the sky.

- **Subject-Verb Agreement**

  blow
  Winter winds usually ~~blows~~ from north to south.

- **Subject-Verb Agreement**

  are
  Sedimentary rocks ~~is~~ made of pieces of rock, minerals,

  or organisms.

- **Subject-Verb Agreement**

  knows   *are*
  Nobody ~~know~~ who invented eyeglasses, but they ~~is~~ very useful.

- **Subject-Verb Agreement**

  spins
  The air in tornadoes ~~spin~~ in a circle.

Proofreading Sentences

History of the Language 1

- **Using the Right Word, Capitalization, Numbers**

  There   26   E
  ~~Their~~ are twenty-six letters in the ~~e~~nglish alphabet.

- **Commas (To Set Off Long Phrases and Clauses), Using the Right Word, Capitalization**

                    their   G
  At one time in ~~they're~~ history, the ~~g~~reeks wrote from right to left.

- **Capitalization, Subject-Verb Agreement**

         S   were
  The ~~s~~emites ~~was~~ the first people to use pictures as words.

- **Capitalization, Commas (To Set Off Appositives)**

         E
  The ~~e~~gyptians invented hieroglyphics, a kind of picture writing, 5,000 years ago.

- **Capitalization, Subject-Verb Agreement**

                          use S   I
  Today, deaf people ~~uses~~ ~~s~~ign ~~l~~anguage to talk to other people.

Proofreading Sentences

History of the Language 2

- **Using the Right Word, Irregular Verbs, Capitalization**

  The *E*/~~e~~nglish language was ~~spoke~~ *spoken* only ~~buy~~ *by* people in England in the 1500s.

- **Contractions, Commas (To Set Off Long Clauses)**

  Because ~~its~~ *it's* spoken throughout the world⌃*,* English is being called the first global language.

- **Hyphens, Using the Right Word, Irregular Verbs**

  Three ⌃*-* fourths of the world's ~~male~~ *mail* today is ~~wrote~~ *written* in English.

- **Possessives, Numbers, Adjectives (Superlative)**

  Of all the ~~worlds~~ *world's* two thousand ~~and~~ seven hundred *2,700* languages, English has the ~~most~~ richest vocabulary.

- **Numbers, Subject-Verb Agreement**

  The English language ~~have~~ *has* over five hundred thousand *500,000* words while German ~~have~~ *has* only one hundred ~~and~~ eighty-five thousand *185,000* words.

Proofreading Sentences

Animal Crackers 1

● **Commas (To Set Off Interjections), Numbers, Using the Right Word**

Wow*,* a female herring ~~lies~~ *lays* ~~30 thousand~~ *30,000* eggs at once!

● **Using the Right Word, Possessives**

Did you ~~no~~ *know* that the ~~mail~~ *male* sea horse protects the ~~mothers~~ *mother's*

eggs by keeping them in a pouch on his stomach?

● **Commas (To Set Off Appositives), Using the Right Word**

One very unusual fish*,* the flounder*,* has both eyes on one

side of ~~it's~~ *its* body.

● **Using the Right Word, Plurals**

The archerfish knocks insects off ~~there~~ *their* ~~leafs~~ *leaves* by shooting them

with a stream of water.

● **Commas (To Separate Adjectives), Using the Right Word, Commas (Between Two Independent Clauses)**

Tropical fish must live in clear*,* warm water*,* or they will ~~dye~~ *die*.

Proofreading Sentences

Animal Crackers 2

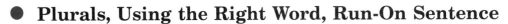

- ## Plurals, Using the Right Word, Run-On Sentence

  Kangaroos

  ~~Kangarooes~~ can really jump. *L*/large ones can cover more ~~then~~ *than* 30

  feet with one leap!

- ## Adjectives (Superlative), Capitalization

  My golden *r*/Retriever is the ~~most~~ *calmest* ~~calm~~ dog in all of *D*/dade

  C/county.

- ## Double Subject, Using the Right Word

  Female black widow spiders ~~they~~ sometimes kill *their* ~~there~~ mates.

- ## Using the Right Word, Subject-Verb Agreement

  see

  A few animals ~~sea~~ in color, but most animals only *see* ~~sees~~ shades

  of gray.

- ## Colon, Using the Right Word, Commas (In a Series)

  made

  Movies have been ~~maid~~ about the following dogs: Lassie, Snoopy,

  Marmaduke, and Beethoven.

Proofreading Sentences

Maps, Maps, Maps 1

● **Commas (To Set Off Long Phrases and in Addresses), Plurals, Capitalization**

According to my map of the United States**,** there are many
cities
~~citys~~ in Florida that are ~~W~~est of Cleveland**,** Ohio.
(*w* above the *W* in West)

● **Using the Right Word, Subject-Verb Agreement, Plurals**

Seas ~~is~~ (*are*) large ~~bodys~~ (*bodies*) of salt water partly surrounded ~~buy~~ (*by*) land.

● **Quotation Marks, Using the Right Word**

Mr. Baily said, **"**Look up the Galapagos Islands on ~~you're~~ (*your*)
maps and ~~right~~ (*write*) down ~~there~~ (*their*) latitude and longitude.**"**

● **Capitalization, Run-On Sentence** *(Answers may vary.)*

In 1849 a great flood of settlers headed west**.** ~~t~~hey followed (*T*)
the map of ~~o~~regon and ~~c~~alifornia made in 1848. (*O*, *C*)

● **Commas (To Set Off Long Phrases and Clauses), Using the Right Word**

When tiny sea creatures leave ~~they're~~ (*their*) skeletons behind**,** coral
is ~~maid~~ (*made*).

Proofreading Sentences

Maps, Maps, Maps 2

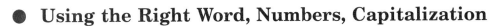

● **Using the Right Word, Numbers, Capitalization**

There are   *7,100*
They're over ~~seven thousand one hundred~~ islands that make up
                                   P
the country called the philippines.

● **Using the Right Word, Capitalization**

                    e   *w*   *through*
The equator goes from East to West and passes ~~threw~~ South

America and Africa.

● **Capitalization, Sentence Fragment**

                             S   *It's t*
Did you know that the Caspian sea is actually a lake? The

largest inland saltwater lake in the world.

● **Capitalization, Semicolon**

                                       M   *;*
Wisconsin and Minnesota are states in the midwest Arizona and
N
new Mexico are part of the southwest.

● **Commas (To Set Off Long Phrases and Clauses),
Using the Right Word, End Punctuation**

                                                      capital
Before reading this sentence, did you know that the ~~capitol~~ of
            ?
Canada is Ottawa.

Proofreading Sentences

Maps, Maps, Maps 3

- **Subject-Verb Agreement, Numbers**

  Canada ~~are~~ *is* a large country with a small population of *27 million* ~~27,000,000~~ people.

- **Possessives, Commas (To Keep Numbers Clear), Using the Right Word**

  China's ~~Chinas~~ first emperor was buried with ~~a~~ *an* army of ~~7500~~ *7,500* clay soldiers.

- **Run-On Sentence, Using the Right Word** *(Answers may vary.)*

  The Sahara ~~Dessert~~ *Desert* may be the hottest place on earth; *I*t holds the record temperature of 136.4 degrees Fahrenheit.

- **Using the Right Word, Commas (To Set Off Appositives)**

  The Czech Republic and Slovakia, two of the newest nations in the world, used ~~too~~ *to* be called Czechoslovakia.

- **Commas (To Set Off Clauses), Capitalization**

  When you are at the *N*orth *P*ole, the only direction you can go is *S*outh.

Proofreading Sentences

Maps, Maps, Maps 4

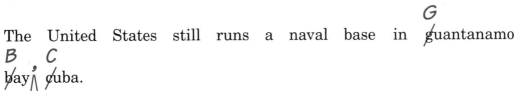

- **Capitalization, Commas (In Addresses)**

    The United States still runs a naval base in $\overset{G}{\text{g}}$uantanamo
    $\overset{B}{\text{b}}$ay$\overset{C}{,}$ $\overset{}{\text{c}}$uba.

- **Commas (To Set Off Appositives), Capitalization,
  Using the Right Word**

    Luxembourg$\overset{}{,}$ a tiny country in $\overset{E}{\text{e}}$urope$\overset{}{,}$ is only a little larger $\overset{than}{\text{then}}$
    $\overset{R}{\text{r}}$hode $\overset{I}{\text{i}}$sland.

- **Capitalization, Commas (To Set Off Appositives)**

    The $\overset{S}{\text{s}}$uez $\overset{C}{\text{c}}$anal$\overset{}{,}$ a waterway constructed from 1859 to 1869$\overset{}{,}$
    connects the $\overset{M}{\text{m}}$editerranean $\overset{S}{\text{s}}$ea to the $\overset{R}{\text{r}}$ed $\overset{S}{\text{s}}$ea.

- **Subject-Verb Agreement, Commas (To Set Off Long Clauses),
  Capitalization**

    If you $\overset{were}{\text{was}}$ traveling between $\overset{O}{\text{o}}$gden and $\overset{P}{\text{p}}$rovo$\overset{}{,}$ which state would

    you be in?

- **Capitalization, Using the Right Word**

    The Amazon $\overset{R}{\text{r}}$iver contains more water $\overset{than}{\text{then}}$ the Nile $\overset{R}{\text{r}}$iver,

    the Mississippi $\overset{R}{\text{r}}$iver, and the Yangtze $\overset{R}{\text{r}}$iver put together.

Proofreading Sentences

Colors, Signs, and Symbols 1

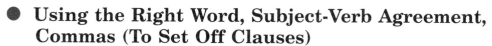

- **Using the Right Word, Subject-Verb Agreement, Commas (To Set Off Clauses)**

  know
  As all artists ~~no~~, chosing the ~~write~~ right colors for painting ~~are~~ is

  important.

- **Commas (In a Series), Irregular Verbs**

  took
  The artist ~~taked~~ red, yellow, and blue paints and mixed

  them to make orange, green, and violet.

- **Subject-Verb Agreement, Contractions, Plurals**

  can't
  People who ~~cant~~ tell the difference between ~~colores~~ colors ~~is~~ are

  color-blind.

- **Using the Right Word, Run-On Sentence** *(Answers may vary.)*

  buy   T
  The oranges you ~~by~~ in the store may have been colored; the
  their
  sellers want ~~there~~ fruit to look nice and bright.

- **Commas (Between Two Independent Clauses), Using the Right Word**

  There   no
  ~~Their~~ is ~~know~~ word in the English language that rhymes with

  "orange," but you could put two words together ~~too~~ to make a

  rhyme.

Proofreading Sentences

Colors, Signs, and Symbols 2

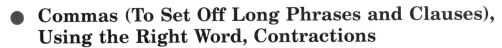

- ### Commas (To Set Off Long Phrases and Clauses), Using the Right Word, Contractions

  If you lived in ancient Rome; you could*nt* where purple unless

  couldn't wear

  you were a member of the emperor's family.

- ### Commas (To Set Off Appositives), Capitalization, Using the Right Word

  At won time in French history, only the ₚPrincess could wear

  one

  scarlet; a bright read color.

  red

- ### Using the Right Word, Contractions, Plurals

  Because they're were no sidewalkes long ago, theyd roll out a

  there   *sidewalks*   *they'd*

  red carpet for the royal family's too walk on.

  families to

- ### Capitalization, Contractions, Double Negative, Run-On Sentence *(Answers may vary.)*

  Betsy Ross didnt never design the american flag; Francis ʜHopkinson

  didn't   A   H

  did that.

- ### Plurals, Numbers, Using the Right Word

  I wonder why most countrys have 3 colores in there flags.

  countries   *three colors*   *their*

Proofreading Sentences

Colors, Signs, and Symbols 3

- **Commas (Between Two Independent Clauses), Subject-Verb Agreement**

    School-crossing signs are yellow, but what color ~~is~~ *are* hospital signs?

- **Using the Right Word, Commas (In a Series)**

    I want my little brother ~~two~~ *to* be safe on his bike, ~~sew~~ *so* I ~~learned~~ *taught* him that red means stop, yellow means caution, and green means go.

- **Commas (To Set Off Long Clauses), Using the Right Word, Hyphens**

    When people go walking at night, they should ~~where~~ *wear* light- colored clothing.

- **Subject-Verb Agreement, Using the Right Word**

    To help keep them safe on the job, construction workers ~~wheres~~ *wear* brightly colored hard hats.

- **Subject-Verb Agreement, Using the Right Word**

    The wires used ~~buy~~ *by* electricians ~~is~~ *are* color coded to prevent accidents and fires.

Proofreading Sentences

U.S. History 1

● **Abbreviations, Numbers**

In ~~nineteen ninety~~ *1990* L. Douglas Wilder became the first

African American governor in the ~~U.S.~~ *United States*

● **Commas (Between Two Independent Clauses),**
Using the Right Word, Capitalization

We all ~~no~~ *know* the first president of the ¢nited *U* ¢tates *S* ; but do you

know the first vice president?

● **Commas (To Set Off Appositives), Capitalization, Irregular Verbs**

George Washington ; the first president of the ¢nited *U* States ; was

~~sweared~~ *sworn* into office in New York City.

● **Run-On Sentence, Irregular Verbs** *(Answers may vary.)*

The first American train robbery ~~taked~~ *took* place in 1866 . *T* ¢he robbers

made off with $16,000.

● **Using the Right Word, Italics (Underlining), Capitalization**

Thomas Paine helped ¢mericans *A* understand the true meaning of

freedom by ~~righting~~ *writing* <u>The Age of Reason</u> and other books.

Proofreading Sentences

U.S. History 2

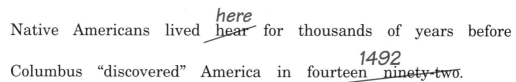

● **Using the Right Word, Numbers**

Native Americans lived ~~hear~~ *here* for thousands of years before Columbus "discovered" America in fourteen ~~ninety-two~~ *1492*.

● **Capitalization, Numbers, Commas (In Addresses), Run-On Sentence** *(Answers may vary.)*

The first *S* ~~s~~panish colony in America was established in Pensacola, Florida, in 1559. *I* ~~i~~t lasted only *two* ~~2~~ years.

● **Commas (To Set Off Long Phrases or Clauses), Capitalization, Using the Right Word**

After many years of debate, the South decided to ~~brake~~ *break* away from the Union and form the *C* ~~c~~onfederate *S* ~~s~~tates of *A* ~~a~~merica.

● **Capitalization, Using the Right Word, Commas (In Addresses)**

The *C* ~~c~~onfederate *S* ~~s~~tates of America established ~~there~~ *their* capital in *R* ~~r~~ichmond, *V* ~~v~~irginia.

● **Capitalization, Run-On Sentence, Irregular Verbs, Using the Right Word** *(Answers may vary.)*

General Robert E. Lee ~~lead~~ *led* the army for the *S* ~~s~~outh. Ulysses S. Grant ~~become~~ *became* the top general for the *N* ~~n~~orth.

Proofreading Sentences

Science and Inventions 1

- ### Commas (Between Independent Clauses), Using the Right Word, Colon

  We had science class at 10̲30 this morning in the park, and
  Mr. Bartz learned *(taught)* us how to tell the age of trees.

- ### Numbers, Commas (To Set Off Long Phrases and Clauses), Capitalization

  After walking in space *(five)* 5 times, astronauts were able to repair
  the *(H)* hubble telescope.

- ### Subject-Verb Agreement, Using the Right Word

  The extinction of dinosaurs *(was)* were probably caused by a meteorite
  (that) who hit the earth.

- ### Numbers, Possessives, Irregular Verbs

  The *(dinosaurs')* dinosaurs extinction *(took)* taked place about *(65 million)* 65,000,000 years ago.

- ### Using the Right Word, Subject-Verb Agreement

  Some people still wonder *(whether there)* weather their ever *(were)* was any dinosaurs.

Proofreading Sentences

Science and Inventions 2

● **Capitalization, Hyphens, Possessives**

At certain times during the Ice ~~age~~ $\overset{A}{}$, one $\overset{-}{\wedge}$ third of the
$\overset{earth's}{\underline{\text{earths}}}$ surface was covered with ice.

● **Commas (Between Independent Clauses), Double Subject, Using the Right Word**

The earth ~~it~~ is made of many layers$\overset{,}{\wedge}$ and the heaviest
$\overset{metals}{\underline{\text{medals}}}$ are at the center.

● **Commas (Between Independent Clauses), Contractions, Subject-Verb Agreement**

The interior of the earth $\overset{gets}{\underline{\text{get}}}$ hot enough to melt rock$\overset{,}{\wedge}$ and
$\overset{that's}{\underline{\text{thats}}}$ how lava $\overset{is}{\underline{\text{are}}}$ formed.

● **Numbers, Adjectives (Superlative)**

The ~~most~~ oldest rock ever found is almost $\overset{4\ billion}{\underline{\text{4,000,000,000}}}$

years old!

● **Using the Right Word, Run-On Sentence, Possessives**
(Answers may vary.)

Glaciers are large blocks of moving ice$\overset{.\ S}{\wedge}$ sometimes $\overset{pieces}{\underline{\text{peaces}}}$
$\overset{break}{\underline{\text{brake}}}$ off at the $\overset{ocean's}{\underline{\text{oceans}}}$ edge $\overset{to}{\underline{\text{too}}}$ form icebergs.

Proofreading Sentences

Science and Inventions 3

● **Commas (To Set Off Appositives),
Using the Right Word**

Willis Carrier, a scientist from New York, invented the first *air* ~~heir~~

conditioner.

● **Hyphens, Commas (To Set Off Appositives and in Addresses)**

The first air-conditioned building, a movie theater, was located in

Chicago, Illinois.

● **Using the Right Word, Commas (To Set Off Appositives),
Periods**

Philo T. Farnsworth, the father of television, invented the electronic

device that *made* ~~maid~~ television possible.

● **Capitalization, Sentence Fragment** *(Answers may vary.)*

In 1929 Vladimir *K*. Zworykin invented the first electronic

t *He was a* *A*
Television system. ~~A~~ Russian-born american.

● **Using the Right Word, Commas (To Set Off Interruptions)**

seen
The first picture ~~scene~~ on television was, believe it or not,

Felix the Cat.

Proofreading Sentences

Literature and Life 1

- **Possessives, Using the Right Word**

  Sir Gawain is the ~~night~~ _knight_ of King ~~Arthurs~~ _Arthur's_ court who ~~excepts~~ _accepts_

  the Green ~~Knights~~ _Knight's_ challenge to battle.

- **Commas (To Set Off Appositives), Irregular Verbs, Subject-Verb Agreement**

  The Beatles ~~broked~~ _broke_ up in 1970, the year my aunt ~~were~~ _was_ born.

- **Commas (To Set Off Appositives), Sentence Error (Confusing "Of" for "Have"), Using the Right Word**

  You would ~~of~~ _have_ liked The Nutcracker, the ~~tail~~ _tale_ of a girl who

  dreams of the land of the Sugar Plum Fairy.

- **Commas (In Dates and Addresses), Sentence Fragment**

  Michael Jackson _was_ born in Gary, Indiana, on August 29, 1958.

- **Commas (To Set Off Appositives), Capitalization**

  Agatha Christie, a famous mystery writer, created the first

  female detective, _M_miss Jane Marple.

Proofreading Sentences

Literature and Life 2

● **Commas (To Set Off Long Phrases and Clauses), Italics (Underlining Titles), Capitalization**

In the book ~~c~~harlie *(C)* and the ~~c~~hocolate *(C)* ~~f~~actory *(F)*, Charlie finds a

winning ticket in a Whipple-Scrumptious Fudgemallow Delight

candy bar.

● **Using the Right Word, Possessives**

Did you ~~no~~ *know* that boy collies were used to play Lassie because

the male ~~dogs~~ *dogs'* coats stay shiny all year?

● **Commas (To Set Off Interjections), Using the Right Word, Run-On Sentence** *(Answers may vary.)*

Wow, ~~their~~ *there* are 47 strings on a harp. I wouldn't have guessed that.

● **Quotation Marks (For Special Words), Using the Right Word**

"Humble" is the last word that Charlotte ~~rights~~ *writes* in her web.

● **Commas (In a Series), Capitalization, Using the Right Word, Numbers**

Butterfinger, ~~a~~lmond *(A)* ~~j~~oy *(J)*, and ~~f~~ifth *(F)* ~~a~~venue *(A)* are just ~~3~~ *three* of the many

kinds of ~~C~~andy *(c)* ~~B~~ars *(b)* to ~~chose~~ *choose* from.

Proofreading Sentences

Literature and Life 3

- ## Commas (Between Independent Clauses),
  ## Commas (To Set Off Interruptions)

  Superheroes are , of course , very powerful , and the Power

  Rangers are superpowerful.

- ## Capitalization, Commas (In a Series), Subject-Verb Agreement

  Both ~~s~~uperman and ~~s~~uperwoman i~~s~~ still popular in comics ,

  movies , and television.

  S *S* *are*

- ## Possessives, Capitalization

  In ~~c~~hild of the ~~o~~wl, Casey~~s~~ ~~g~~randmother Paw-Paw lives in

  ~~c~~hinatown.

  C *O* *Casey's* *g*
  C

- ## Using the Right Word, Commas (To Set Off Long Clauses)

  When he needed a ~~brake~~ , Sherlock Holmes ~~learned~~ himself to

  play the violin.

  break *taught*

- ## Using the Right Word, Subject-Verb Agreement,
  ## Italics (Underlining Titles)

  <u>Pippi Longstocking</u> is a book about a spunky girl who can

  lift a horse and ~~don't where~~ shoes or like school.

  doesn't wear

Proofreading Sentences

Literature and Life 4

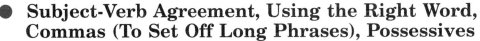

- **Subject-Verb Agreement, Using the Right Word, Commas (To Set Off Long Phrases), Possessives**

  In Lewis Carroll's story about Alice, hedgehogs are used for croquet balls.

- **Commas (To Set Off Interruptions), Using the Right Word**

  Frankenstein is, of course, the scientist who created the monster, not the monster himself.

- **Commas (Between Independent Clauses), Capitalization, Italics (Underlining Titles), Using the Right Word**

  Winnie-the-Pooh made a honey jar into a boat called the Floating Bear, and he sailed away into the rays of the sun.

- **Using the Right Word, Italics (Underlining Titles), Capitalization, Commas (To Set Off Appositives)**

  In 1937 the first Disney movie, Snow White and the Seven Dwarfs, won the hearts of the American people.

- **Italics (Underlining Titles), Using the Right Word, Capitalization, Commas (In Addresses)**

  Home Alone is a movie about a boy who was left behind when his family went to Paris, France.